THE COURAGE TO LOOK BACK

KEEP ON KEEPING ON

THE SEQUEL TO *The Boys of St. Mary's*

CAROLINE WHITEHEAD

By the same author

Shadows In Every Corner

Surviving The Shadows

Rowland: A Heart of Sunshine

Under The Old Railway Clock

The Boys of St. Mary's: Keep On Keeping On (Editor)

THE COURAGE TO LOOK BACK
KEEP ON KEEPING ON

THE SEQUEL TO *The Boys of St. Mary's*

Stories by:
Delvin John Flynn
The late Patrick Heffernan
John Michael Murray
Antony Hayman
Michael Gormley
and
other members of the KOKO St. Mary's old boys "network."

EDITED BY
CAROLINE WHITEHEAD

PUBLISHING HOUSE

Canada   www.agiopublishing.com

© 2017, Caroline Whitehead. Stories and
photographs used by permission of the authors.
All rights reserved.
Without limiting the rights under copyright reserved above,
no part of this publication may be reproduced, stored
in or introduced into a retrieval system, or transmitted,
in any form or by any means (electronic, mechanical,
photocopying, recording or otherwise), without the prior
written permission of both the copyright owner(s) and the
publisher of this book.

The Courage To Look Back
ISBN 978-1-927755-62-4 (paperback)
ISBN 978-1-927755-63-1 (ebook)

Cataloguing information available from
Library and Archives Canada.
Printed on acid-free paper.
Agio Publishing House is a socially responsible company,
measuring success on a triple-bottom-line basis.

10 9 8 7 6 5 4 3 2 1b

DEDICATION

To the old boys of St. Mary's,
Gravesend, Kent,
and especially to the child migrants
shipped to Australia in 1953
who never came back.

What lies behind us
and what lies before us
Are tiny matters compared to
what lies within us.

~ Ralph Waldo Emerson

ACKNOWLEDGEMENTS

Special thanks and appreciation to (Delvin) John Flynn for his encouragement to keep alive the old boys network, formed by him July 1988 – which celebrates its Thirtieth Anniversary July 2018.

To Terry McKenna for his time and energy to collect and compile the group's emails, photographs and other pertinent material from (Delvin) John Flynn, and to ensure safe delivery between continents so this publication was made possible.

To Mavis Heffernan of Australia, who generously allowed us to publish her late husband's memoirs, we extend our sincere thanks and appreciation.

To members of the writing group of the old boys of St. Mary's, Gravesend, Kent who approved publication of their emails from 2015 to 2017 and stories of past eras by Agio Publishing House, Victoria, British Columbia, Canada.

To my son-in-law Don Boston for his invaluable time and expertise to keep all technical systems on my computer smoothly running.

To AccessCopyright and Canada Council For The Arts who generously support eligible Canadian affiliate writers, we appreciate their financial support and recognition.

To Bruce and Marsha Batchelor, Agio Publishing House, Victoria, BC. for their advice and support to make this publication possible. The cover design is by award-winning graphic designer Marsha Batchelor.

— Caroline Whitehead

CONTENTS

Special Tribute To (Delvin) John Flynn	i
Introduction: Lost Boys' Story *by David Crisp*	iii
About This Book	v
The History of St. Mary's	vii
St. Mary's School For Boys, Parrock Road, Gravesend *by John Flynn*	ix
Emails From The KOKO Group – 2015	1
First *Contact* News Letter (December 1954)	21
The Army And You *by Leslie Hayes*	25
Contact #2, February 1955	27
KOKO Group Emails, *cont'd*	31
Contact #3, June 1955	41
Contact #4, August 1955	49
KOKO Emails, *cont'd*	55
Memories Of St. Mary's, Gravesend *by Patrick Heffernan*	69
The Skylark On Windmill Hill *by John Michael Murray*	74
Life After St. Mary's *by Antony Hayman*	80
Child Migrant *by Michael Gormley*	92
Photo Album	97
Emails from the KOKO Writing Group – 2016 & 2017	105
Epilogue	237

John and his wife Josie with grandson Joseph

SPECIAL TRIBUTE TO (DELVIN) JOHN FLYNN

In July 1988, (Delvin) John Flynn came up with the plan to formulate a "network" of the old boys of St. Mary's Orphanage, Gravesend, Kent, and to preserve for all time the history of its beginnings. His idea was to encourage past residents who had long left the orphanage, some to join the Armed Forces, others who were shipped to Australia and Canada under the Commonwealth Flag, and to those who migrated to live in another land far away as possible from the shores of England, its pastoral lands, and memories of childhood – encouraging them to merge together and one day to recall their memories and friendship as the old boys of St. Mary's.

Delvin was not to realize at this time how profoundly this would effect so many. Nor did he anticipate how much fortitude and perseverance would be required. Nevertheless, following his personal motto of KOKO (keep on keeping on), he contacted Irena Lyczkowska of Cabrini for details of any knowledge of the whereabouts of the old boys whose personal files were held in their archives [these file were later transferred to The Diagrama Foundation in 2015]. Irena's response was positive. She said she was willing to help in every way. The names of some of the boys who were still in touch and kept on file at Cabrini, she handed over to Delvin.

Delvin's next move was to open up a dialogue on the Orpington Message Board to find if those old boys who were "shuffled" out of St. Mary's to the care of Christian Brothers at St. Josephs, Orpington were still alive. His message resulted in my connection to him, as his message referred to the two orphanages of which I was most familiar at Orpington, Kent. Henceforth, a friendship developed and since, we have remained in touch.

With the tenacity of the Irish blood flowing through his veins, Delvin was inspired to dig up whatever history he could find on the Blackheath Hostel, the Bletchingly Farm in Godstone, Surrey and to write letters to the various Catholic authorities, bishops and other clergy to extract this past history and to forward it to his steadily growing network of the old boys of St. Mary's.

In 2015, the many years of emails from the KOKO members, with the exception of those of a personal nature for Delvin's eyes only, were compiled in a book under the title *The Boys of St. Mary's: Keep On Keeping On*. This brought many more of the old boys out of the woodwork, some from different parts of the world who now are frequent writers to the KOKO group; a few of whom have gradually "opened up" to tell their personal stories of childhood experiences.

This unique network now includes close to forty members from all walks of life, and many of the old boys who live far away as Australia, Canada, Germany and other parts of Europe regularly keep in touch. The camaraderie is second to none; each and every member (honorary, as myself) have over the past thirty years developed a tight-knit relationship to support, encourage and most of all, keep on keeping on. An astounding achievement.

It is with pride to look back at (Delvin) John Flynn's foresight in 1988, to see a future ahead, and to forge together his network of old boys and inspire them to write about their personal memories *with the courage to look back.*

IN THIS SPECIAL TRIBUTE TO OUR FOUNDER, WE WISH TO EXTEND OUR WARMEST AND APPRECIATIVE THANKS FOR HIS GENEROUS TIME, ENERGY AND LOVE THE PAST THIRTY YEARS. HE HAS SUCCESSFULLY ACHIEVED HIS GOAL TO BRING TOGETHER THE "NETWORK" OF THE MEMBERS OF KOKO.

FROM ALL OF US, WHO CELEBRATE OUR THIRTIETH ANNIVERSARY JULY 2018, WITH LOVE AND GREAT AFFECTION, THE KOKO GROUP OF ST. MARY'S, GRAVESEND, KENT.

INTRODUCTION

LOST BOYS' STORY

An orphanage was not too bad to live in for the little boys lost to society, without a trace, without a mother or father to guide them, and no one else to look up to or rely on. We had smiles, as little boys usually do. But then the *Men in Black* arrived on cue. They changed our lives completely around.

Dreams, hopes and ambition now ran aground. We grew up as men in our new home out of town when we left. We went out on our own with a frown into the big wide world we knew nothing about. And life for us was one big clout.

As the years went by some of the boys failed to make it to their twenty-fifth birthday and had no joy. Why did it happen? Their lives were cut short.

Why was there no-one to discuss their hurt? The beer and wine got to them and they had no home to go home to. They were without gems. I think the boys I knew ended up on the streets of a city called Perth, as homeless men some of us do meet. I know a lot of my friends have gone now and one day I think I will be with them again somehow.

Many of them with a new life; I miss them all, as life cuts like a knife. I think I was a lucky one. I came through hard times and difficulties with the world askew. For them I will keep going on as long as I live, and trust in my heart I find a morsel of peace and forgive.

— *David Crisp* – 1st December 1944 to 9th April 2015. R.I.P.

ABOUT THIS BOOK

This sequel to *The Boys of St. Mary's* is made possible through the generosity of the members of the old boys network worldwide who allowed their ongoing emails from 2015 to the early part of 2017 to be published by Agio Publishing House, Victoria, British Columbia, Canada.

It is also at a poignant time to pay a Special Tribute to (Delvin) John Flynn. His foresight to form a network in July 1988, nearly thirty years ago and with his motto to Keep On Keeping On, was to hope and to encourage the old boys of St. Mary's, Gravesend, Kent to keep in touch.

Due to the publication in 2015 of the first book of past memoirs, many surprises for the network were yet to unfold. When they became known little did Flynn realize the magnitude of his motto KOKO and how it was to spread far afield to all corners of the globe.

Those who had long left St. Mary's, perhaps with thoughts of untying the "umbilical cord" of life in an orphanage, were to astound Flynn when they became aware of the network and were to read the stories of past friends in *The Boys of St. Mary's*. Their immediate response was to get in touch with the network, sending not only the history of their memories, but also old photographs held by them over the years.

Initially when contact was made with Flynn, he found that many of those who came out of the woodwork were reticent to speak of their childhood experiences for reasons known only to themselves. Some of them, today, are still unable to shake the demons of the past from their shoulders.

In time, and with encouragement and through its increased membership, more and more past residents of St. Mary's have surfaced to tell their stories of childhood experiences through the channel of emails.

With fortitude and pride of the motto KOKO, they have connected with school friends who now have the courage to look back.

The included emails from a group of writers in England, Australia, Canada and other countries have been kept in their original form, except where this would have made them difficult to read.

Several honorary members of the group who were not connected to St. Mary's include Ann Phyall of England, Caroline Whitehead of Canada, Mavis Heffernan of Australia and Christine Shrosbree of England, who are contributors to the old boys network by courtesy of the group and Mr. Flynn.

THE HISTORY OF ST. MARY'S

FROM THE RECORDS OF (DELVIN) JOHN FLYNN

In the publication of *The Boys of St. Mary's*, little information was available as to the building of the orphanage and its original history and how it all began. Only recently, after hearing a sequel to *Boys* was contemplated, did the history of Mount Milton College come to light through the generosity of Antony Hayman who had held the document of its origin since 2011.

When inquiring to Teresa Downey, late of Cabrini Children's Society about his personal file, she sent him the following letter:

Dated: August 10, 2011.

Dear Antony,
I was pleased to have the opportunity of speaking with you today. I am sending a history of St. Mary's and some photographs which I hope will be of some interest to you.

I will let you know when the records are ready; should be in a couple of weeks, three at the most. Do let me know if you would like me to bring them down. It will be fine. It will also be fine if you wish to receive them through the post.

I have emailed your email address to John Flynn so you should be hearing from him.
Best wishes,
Teresa Downey

PHOTO AND MESSAGE FROM THE POPE

A photograph of Pope Pius Xl was bought by George May, a parishioner of St. Joseph's Catholic Church in Bromley, at a local antique market in early 1999. He immediately recognised the significance of the photograph from the dedication to the Southwark Rescue Society and its new home at Gravesend.

Through the members of Medway Towns Circle of the Catenian Association, George was put in touch with Tony Larkin who is known as the local historian for Gravesend.

The photograph was described to Tony over the phone and he too immediately remembered it – originally it had been displayed at St. Mary's School for Boys, Parrock Road, Gravesend and then passed on to the new houses. Tony was a resident of St. Mary's School in the 1940s and kind enough to pass on the history.

Our grateful thanks go out to all who helped in producing this little booklet and we hope it will bring back happy and nostalgic memories.

The original of the photograph has been suitably framed and returned to the Catholic Children's Society (formerly the Southwark Rescue Society) in Gravesend.

The Pope's message reads: "We bless with all our heart the Southwark Rescue Society and its new home at Gravesend." [Signature and date, ineligible]

ST. MARY'S SCHOOL FOR BOYS
PARROCK ROAD, GRAVESEND

REFLECTIONS (*transcribed out of a historical booklet*)

Milton Mount College, Milton, Kent 1873–1973

The idea of the college originated from Rev. William Guest, Minister of Princes' Street Congregational Church, Gravesend. His inspiration came from Holylake Female Seminar in the USA. Rev. Guest contacted Dr. Kirkdale in Boston, the president of the seminar, who then took it upon himself to found the college for the daughters of congregational ministers, along the lines as Holylake Seminar. He was to find great support from all over the country for the proposed scheme, the final site to be chosen was at Milton, next to Gravesend. The location was considered ideal and the price was described as moderate.

The site for the new college was on a prominent hill, 200 feet above sea level with a spectacular view of the River Thames and across to Essex. Various suggestions were made for the naming of the college, the final choice being "Milton Mount".

Mr. C.E. Robins from Southampton was selected to design the building at a cost of 9,750, Pounds. On the 5th October 1871 Samuel Morley, MP, a great supporter of the scheme, laid the foundation stone.

1873 The college was built to hold 150 girls and the first principal was Miss Selina Hadland, a great friend of Miss Buss, founder of North London Collegiate School for Girls and Miss Beale, founder of Cheltenham Ladies' College. These three ladies were genuine pioneers of women's education and their influence, even today, cannot be fully appreciated.

Miss Hadland, as if foreseeing the coming of the 20th Century, introduced into the college curriculum Chemistry, Science and Physiology, opening up new opportunities in women's education and resulted in three students receiving London BA Degrees. Due to this success the first High School was introduced and later a Technical School for girls and produced excellent academic achievements even by today's standards. Her pioneering work for women's education took its toll and in 1889 Miss Hadland resigned her position with honour.

1889 Miss Ethel Mary Conder, the second Principal, or Headmistress as she preferred to be addressed, was educated under Miss Beale at Cheltenham College and at Girton. She introduced student teachers to help teach the younger girls music in return for free board and residence.

1891 Rev. William Guest died but the college never really honoured him as a founder of the college.

1893 Expansion to the college became necessary as admission was open to all the daughters from local business people and church families. The college purchased the adjoining house and land in Parlour Road, plus the property next door, expanding Milton Mount through to Leith Park Road. The land was to make the college self-sufficient in growing its own fruit and vegetables; it also had its own piggery, known on the map in those days as "Three Tree Hill". The land was also used for botany and natural history lessons and remained as gardens with the piggery until 1955. The playground area is still known, to this day, as "The New Family Units".

1895 It became necessary to establish a Junior School so that the new entrants would be educated to a satisfactory standard. During this year additional entrants were admitted to the college. The High School moved to another site in the area close to Milton Mount College. The four annexes in the town, created in Miss Hadland's days, were centralised by Miss Conder who considered it beneficial to all concerned. The wisdom of Miss Conder was again illustrated when she introduced fire escapes to the building. The college could be cleared of pupils in ten minutes when fire drills became a regular exercise.

1906   Miss Anne Askew Woodall MA, Cambridge, a mathematical tripos and excellent teacher, was appointed as a teacher. She would later become the third Headmistress on Miss Condor's retirement.

1910   Miss Conder resigned partly due to stress, but also realizing that "new blood" (in the form of Miss Woodall) was needed to take the college into the 20th Century.

       Miss Woodall changed the uniform from red to white blouse under navy blue tunics. She also introduced gymnastics, which heralded the first lady gymnastics teacher. Miss Woodall retired in 1926.

1911   The college required further expansion when a reading room and library were introduced.

1914   Although serious problems had arisen over the years, nothing compared with the outbreak of the war when Gravesend was one of the first places to be bombed by Zeppelins.

1915   Bombs dropped on Windmill Hill in June of that year; therefore, the College and other schools in the area were moved to safer areas of the country. The College building was rented by Vickers, Maxim & Co. to carry out their war work for the neighbouring town of Dartford. Milton Mounts pupils and staff settled at the Royal Agricultural College in Cirencester.

1918 Milton Mount College was requisitioned by the Admiralty for use as a Naval Hospital. The future for Milton Mount ever returning to Gravesend was bleak but, on reflection, as far back as 1893 the college had always been deemed too small for its needs and, although moving to larger premises was always on the agenda, finances would not permit. Although the area was no longer a pleasant rural location, local prominent dignitaries for years used the land for all their sporting activities.

1920 Milton Mount bought Worth Park, Crawley, from Sir Francis Montefoiore for 30,000 pounds and in this year the new college was established.

1921 The college made a claim for damages amounting to 73,000 pounds, the Admiralty appealed and in 1924 the final settlement for compensation was assessed at 35,000 pounds plus costs and possession of the Gravesend building.

1925 St. Mary's School, the Catholic Rescue Society in Milton, closed homes in the area around London as far down as Mottingham in Kent and went on to purchase Milton Mount College to be used as an orphanage.

1926 The orphanage was officially opened and this is when Pope Pius XI sent his portrait signed with his blessings to the new children's home. With approximately 250 boys (300 if necessary) the orphanage/school settled down in their new home which was to be run by the Sisters of Charity (St. Vincent De Paul), a Priest and staff. The boys and school were made welcome to the town, and the Mayor, Mayoress and Councillors were among the guests at the official opening. From a generally quiet beginning the school was to become locally and nationally famous for its exploits in the world of sport, especially football. So great was St. Mary's Boys in the 1930s, their football team, at one time, went three years without losing a match. Other years very rarely did they lose. There were no local trophies but teams from all over came to challenge the boys with little or no success. Also, the same in the amateur boxing world, the boys were regularly in the finals for national championships. All this added to the genuine popularity and pride of their adopted home and town. The people took the school to their hearts with pride and the crowds supporting the Boys boasted a larger attendance than the local football teams (Northfleet – at this time nursery team for Tottenham Hotspur). The town was generally proud of their boys whose success continued through to 1938. It must be mentioned that to mark the Jubilee year of 1935 the local council discussed gifts to be given to all children but decided against it, with one exception: St. Mary's Boys at the orphanage. This occasion was attended by the Mayor.

1939 World War II broke out and all Gravesend children were evacuated for their safety. Sister Bernard (Superior) with other Sisters and staff, like mother hens gathered the boys together where they sailed across to Essex and on through to Suffolk, Norfolk and Cambridge, literally passed from pillar to post trying to find accommodation but without real success as the Sisters would not allow their cares to be split up. Generally a traumatic time for all involved, yet, from this trauma, were a number of reports full of praise for the Sisters and more for the boys from people during their travels commending them on their behaviour and manners in general.

Finally, the problem of a home for the boys and staff came to the notice of Lord and Lady Clifford, who generously offered St. Mary's their home at Ugbrooke Park, Chuddleigh in Devon for the duration of the war. This was a very happy time away from the horrors of the war, plus living in a beautiful house and countryside, with so much space to run around in.

This remained so through until December 1945, when school was returned to Gravesend and all were welcomed back to the home by the Mayor.

St. Mary's building, during the war, was used by the Civil Defence and Home Guard, but sadly, neglect had caused serious and expensive damage and drainage problems. Yet the main thing to the school and the local people was "their Boys were home". The kindness and support of friends and benefactors cannot ever be repaid and so remains just a happy memory.

1946 A memorial plate dedicated to the boys who gave their lives for their country, was erected and paid for by the Old Boys.

1947 Was a hard year for the school during a bitterly cold winter, followed by an outbreak of scarlet fever and then later a measles epidemic. One must mention Dr. Charles Outred who cared for all the school's medical problems but was also a benefactor and true friend of the school.

After the war, football again was to play a prominent role in the life of St. Mary's. Again with guest appearances of Alex James, the team attracted many supporters. The boys played with great skill and enthusiasm and as before the war, was a most successful team. After the war, boxing was not encouraged by the Sisters as it was considered too aggressive and physical.

St. Mary's Boys owe so much to Richard Aloysius Roche for their sporting achievements. Richard came from Ireland to St. Mary's in the 1930s and remained with the school when evacuated to Ugbrooke Park. He stayed with the school until 1951, the year that St. Mary's ceased to be a school. He became manager of Gravesend and Northfleet Football Club for a year, creating in that short time, a team for future success. His vocation was not in professional football and he finally worked with children in need in the Medway area. He was an unassuming man, a kind yet firm and fair schoolmaster, and brilliant at encouraging his boys, whether in education or sport. Many St. Mary's boys again owe a great debt of honour to a wonderful gentleman. This, at the time of his death, was the compliment his many sporting friends from his Gravesend days said of him.

1951 More dramatic changes occurred. St. Mary's School closed and the pupils were transferred to the newly opened Catholic School of St. John's at Denton. In doing so, they were to join the reality of the world. St. Mary's had successful pupils attending St. Joseph's Academy, Blackheath and others going to the Technical School at Gravesend.

Other changes occurred in encouraging more adoption policies and after 1954 saw the ending of institutional life in an orphanage. The introduction of self-contained homes helped prevent young families being split and losing contact with each other. Sister Gerard must always be remembered for her hard and perhaps heart-breaking problems that occurred in introducing the more human liberal policies. She should always be remembered for her work for God and his Children, which all fell into place before she finally left St. Mary's and Gravesend.

The Orchard Gardens, Piggery and Playground, developed into new family-orientated homes; these rightly dedicated to Our Lady, Patroness of St. Mary's School and Home.

Gradually, St. Mary's Home became more and more empty. With this in mind, it was arranged by word of mouth that in 1959 the first and last reunion of old boys, both pre and post wars were to meet and swap their memories. But more to honour and thank the Sisters of Charity for their love and service of the boys, through hard time, yet protected their boys from all their worst evils. Honoured guest was Fr. Paul H. Baker, Priest and teacher for St. Mary's from Ugbrooke Park days through to 1952/3, a good and kind man. Like Mr. Roche, a firm but fair man and loved by the boys and if there were a Priests' roll of honours list it would include Fr. McCrea, Fr. Healey (later Bishop), Fr. Arbuthnott (later Canon) and Fr. Connelly (later Canon) all to have good and caring influences with the boys even after they left St. Mary's. The boys were most grateful for the devotion of the Priests to their personal problems.

The Sisters of Charity became Daughters of Charity, and gradually dwindled in numbers once new homes at Glen View were built. More lay workers moved in to take over control of homes, still with six Sisters living in the homes at the time. A local "Heritage Society" recognised that the Sisters had been in Gravesend for 60 years (Diamond Jubilee) in 1986. The Society presented the Sisters and home with a financial gift and framed picture of the old St. Mary's; none of the Sisters around in 1986 had ever seen the orphanage/Milton Mount. This Society had a soft spot for St. Mary's as they reprinted an old Gravesend Book on General Gordon for the anniversary of his death in 1985. This book was dedicated to the Sisters of St. Mary's, Milton and with other local charities were to be presented with all royalties from the book. This Society's final gesture was to be another donation, to mark the departure of the Sisters from Gravesend on 29th June 1989. A thanksgiving Mass led by Bishop H. Tripp concelebrated with Canon E. Mundy and his curate from St. John's, Gravesend, special guests being the Mayor and Mayoress of Gravesend (Gravesham), leading Borough Officers, Sisters of the Order, "Daughters of Charity" in England and many friends, benefactors, former staff and workers from the old St. Mary's days.

The Sisters came to the borough in 1925 very quietly and in 1989 left as they came, unnoticed, knowing that they had successfully completed God's work in Gravesend, Kent and there were new and more needy pastures for them to continue God's work. The last Sister to leave was Sister Patricia in September of 1989.

Note: This reprint of the booklet, undated and unsigned by the author, has not been changed in content.

EMAILS FROM THE KOKO GROUP – 2015

PICTURE QUERY

Does anyone know where this picture was taken?

Tony Kelly, Toronto, Canada.

Tony,

I believe it was taken in the early 1970s in the large refectory when St. Mary's was due to close. In the foreground Terry Russell is on the left with Tony Sayers on the right. John McKeown is far right. The Duttons are also there, as is John O'Brien.

KOKO.

John

Hi Gang

Tony Kelly Here. I think I was at St. Mary's from 1950 but I know I left in 1956. I worked in the refectory the last couple of years as I remember some time I had to leave the TV show to get things set up. I think the Sister's name was Bernadette: tall, quiet, good to work for, I enjoyed it there.

I worked in Father Baker's gardens and can remember sitting in his rooms watching the TV set for the Quatermass Experiment… washing his new Morris car, raking the gravel drive.

One evening one boy who disobeyed a Sister and took something from the form room after he was told not to, fell down over the bannisters and cracked open his head. He was never the same even with a plate in his head. Before he was quite normal and a bit of a clown.

I spent a little time sleeping in the kids' dorm and working in the kids' dining room which was managed by a lovely dark-haired young lady who had a room in the corner of the dorm. Did not like it and got moved out.

Got caught smoking with some other boy one time. And I forget the punishment. Used to date a lovely girl at the school but the caretaker found out and made me stop. I remember his words: "No St. Mary's boy is going out with my daughter."

It was a great life, better than home, for sure.

Thank you for all the hard work in KOKO'ing.

Presently in Rome; had to visit the Vatican, you know my Catholic upbringing… wanted to see where all my pennies went.

Tony Kelly

Tony,

Good hearing from you. Glad you are still enjoying life. I trust you did some soul-searching when visiting the Vatican? Hope you are well.

KOKO

Caroline

Hi Tony.

Terry McK here. Thanks for sharing your recollections. It seems about the time I was there too. It's highly likely that as an infant, a young one at that time; I may well have been in the dorm sleeping too! I think you are right about Sister Bernadette; your description rings a bell in my memory. Good to hear about you, Tony.

Vatican City is an amazing place, Tony. Hope the Pope invited you in for a cuppa!

KOKO and enjoy Rome too, Tony.

Terry McKenna

Caroline,

I was speaking to Tony Larkin this morning, and I think it relates to a gathering of the old boys of St. Mary's when the school was closing down and it was a farewell to teaching in that magnificent building. I was not present on that day. The building was demolished in the early '70s.

KOKO Love,

John

SCHOOL REUNION

Hi John,

Reading Caroline's email she has got the wrong date, so I wanted to let you know it is Sunday 23 August for the St. John's school reunion.

Her book sounds interesting: I have read two of her books already.

Christine Shrosbree

John,

Was this taken at the reunion? I ask because of the perceived ages of those pictures. The Sisters fill me with dread even though they're not looking at you.

Glen Cawdeary

Glen,

Come to think of it you may be right – was it a reunion? You will probably be aware the Nuns modernized after the Vatican Council, which ended 50 years ago, and they divested themselves of that heavy RAF Blue Serge Habit and took on a more up to date outfit; still not modern but at least not so strange. The white coronets were discarded for a veil. So that was probably the last picture taken.

Glen, you have to let go of those fears – it was all so long ago. I hope you don't have bad dreams.

KOKO.

John

BINDOON

John,

Surely not all of these boys went to Bindoon? I read a book a couple of years ago about the boys at Bindoon and saw a film about it. It sickened me to my very core....

Ann

AUSTRALIA

Ann,

In answer to your last message the boys didn't move over in one hit but by instalments. But that particular picture conjured up memories of my childhood when we would go en masse to the chapel each day for evening prayers. Like the picture we were just twelve years of age and some from our number were shipped to Australia. It was terrible for those who remained. It was like losing our brothers and we just knew there was no prospect of ever seeing them again.

Now because of modern technology, like Skype and Facetime, it would not have applied. I found one of my mates forty years after believing he was dead. He turned up in Queensland and we occasionally chat by phone.

KOKO and keep smiling and well in spite of everything.

Love,

John & Josie

PALM SPRINGS

Hi John & Josie,

I am sat in Seattle Airport en route to Palm Springs to meet and stay with my brother Max and his wife Susan for a week. 10.05AM here and my connection is not until 12.20.

Caroline and I have sorted the cover for the book which I have to say is looking good. I bought a Rogers sim card in Victoria during my first few days with Caroline before joining the "Jet Set" on my way to California.

Having worked for Tandy in the UK, owned then by USA company Radio Shack, I knew exactly what to buy. I rang Caroline at home in Canada and my brother in the USA and got through to both with no problem at all. Hurrah!

Regards as ever to you and Josie.

KOKO.

Terry McK...

Terry,

Really looking forward to hearing how things went on your holiday and hope everything goes well for the rest of your trip.

KOKO

J.

Fragments, Summer 1949

Colin,

I was reading some old publication regarding the Farm when I saw – from *Fragments*, Summer 1949: 'The boys will answer your questions about their training pay and interests.' It might interest you to hear of Malcolm Bedford's tame squirrel which pops up his sleeve with real affection.

Regards,

J & J

PET ANIMALS

Hi John & Josie,

Thank you for the email regarding my brother Malcolm down at the "Farm" at Bletchingly. He was one of life's characters and was often talked about by people who knew of his passion for animals.

Mr. Cadogan was the superintendent at the Farm before being transferred to the home at Blackheath. He told the story of the chicken who had no feathers and had never laid any eggs and was in a sorry state. Malcolm adopted it and after giving it lots of TLC it became the top layer, often laying eggs with double yolks.

Malcolm's love of animals had started at school where he had a collection of frogs, lizards, mice and rats which he kept in his desk. We had an inspection one day of the gas masks kept in our desks before the wartime. It was discovered the residents of his desk had chewed through the visor window of his mask! He then suffered the appropriate punishment for his misdemeanours.

Malcolm sadly passed way several years ago BUT his many anecdotes live on for all us old boys of St. Mary's.

Regards,

Colin and Eileen Bedford

Dear Reader,

Allow me to pause a while to convey my email to Colin for his recollection of the time his brother Malcolm was held accountable for keeping pets in his school desk. Typing this episode and laughing uncontrollably, I almost fell off my chair. Having recovered my equilibrium, I decided to respond to Colin's email and pass a copy to John.

Colin's reply (February 2017)

Malcolm who sadly passed away, is no longer with us, and was one of life's characters whose memories are always with us. He was a popular boy at St. Mary's. After leaving the Home at Gravesend he went to the training farm at Bletchingly in Surrey and the ex-manager told him one of the chickens at the farm was not laying any eggs and was losing its feathers so they called it Gandhi, so was due for the chop! Malcolm came to hear of this and he requested to reprieve the chicken from the imminent execution as it was the chicken's last chance to survive the inevitable to its life.

Malcolm took Gandhi under his wing (excuse the pun) and within a few weeks of tender loving care the chicken had put on weight, regained all its feathers, and became the pride of the run and was the top layer, laying eggs with double yokes.

Permission of the author.

Caroline

Colin

A marvellous story of a great character. Hardly any stories emanated from the Big House (the hostel) compared with the Farm. Circulars and news sheets were regularly sent from the Farm to the boys doing their National Service round the World; encouraging them to maintain contact with one another and with the Farm. Sadly such good work was NOT replicated from those in charge at Blackheath.

Colin, did I mention the boys of the hostel have been airbrushed out of history? The Blackheath RC Church produced a magazine some years go to celebrate its first hundred years and no mention was made of the hostel. One can glean information of the use of the hostel before and after the boys left but not a thing about the boys who lived there. A glaring omission, don't you think?

Regards to you and your long-serving wife Eileen.

KOKO

J & J

Hi John & Josie,

Well, here in a lovely sunny afternoon in Sidney, BC, the temperature is about 20°C by the harbourside. The vista is so pretty and calming. Despite my "problems" walking, it isn't a problem because the thoughtful Canadians provide seating every twenty or thirty yards. I actually feel quite young! Because this is obviously a haven for retired seniors and I have never seen so many zimmers/walkers on the move at once. Caroline is with her daughter and husband today. Of course I was invited but I said, 'not today' because I believe she should have some family time with them and not to worry about me. So here I am sat in the beautiful weather chatting to the very friendly "natives". When they hear an English accent (I gave up trying to tell them it is actually a British one) they love to come over and chat; and you know how shy and reserved I am! Off to Tim Horton's for some coffee shortly.

KOKO for now.

Terry McK.

BOYS HOSTEL, BLACKHEATH

Colin and Eileen,

I propose sending the email below but before I do I shall be pleased if you would scan the details for accuracy. If all appears in order I will copy to the rest of the group.

Best wishes to you and Eileen.

(Delvin) John

Dear Monsignor Nicholas Rothon,

My purpose in writing is to acquaint you with an important part of your church's history. I could have telephoned you but have decided to give you the opportunity to reflect on an event that happened some years ago. I had a request from what was then the Catholic Children's Society at 49 Russell Hill in Purley, Surrey, to assist them in finding any information about a Boys Hostel in Blackheath. The result: A gift from a Fr. Francis Hartley of a booklet published to celebrate the Centenary of Our Lady Help of the Christians church 1873–1973. When I examined this booklet I was very surprised no mention was made of the Boys or the Hostel. This hostel was used to accommodate boys who having reached the age of 25 years left St. Mary's and St. Joseph's Orphanages to enter paid employment. They usually stayed until they entered the Armed Forces to do their National Service. The hostel was in use during the years from the 1940s to the middle of the 1960s after which the premises were put to another use. The boys' spiritual needs would have been served by the clergy of Our Lady Help Christian church and the Priest caring for these boys was I believe Fr. Frank Davis.

Another Priest who participated in the history of the Parish was Fr. Howard Tripp who was later created an assistant Bishop of the Diocese.

Both served as assistant Priests during this period but not at the same time. I can only assume the omission on this part of the church's history was an oversight, since the work carried out at that time of caring for spiritual needs could have enhanced the reputation of your church.

I tried from different directions to learn about the hostel, including contacting the Lewisham Borough Council, but since the hostel was supported by charitable donations they had no remit to oversee the premises. They did however give me a little bit of information about the premises before it was used as a Boys Hostel. I even spoke to Bishop Henderson who was totally unaware of this part of your history and I believe was actually living in the former hostel building.

It will not be long before you celebrate 150 years of the church's presence in the area and you may want to include this into the official history. For your information we have a number of boys who stayed at the hostel and who are members of our writing group and are interested to learn if this email evokes any response.

Sincerely.

(Delvin) John Flynn

Hi John & Josie,

With reference to your email regarding the Blackheath Hostel, the church in question came under the Greenwich Council and not the Lewisham Council as did the hostel. At my time there the parish Priest was Father Loman whose only contact with the hostel was to complain about the boys, including myself, mainly for petty misdemeanours. My wife and I were married at this church not by Father Loman but by Canon Arbuthnott. Because I was getting married to a Non-Catholic my wife had to attend a religious course that was mandatory then. She never completed the course because Fr. Loman dismissed her when she began asking awkward questions of the Catholic Faith. I think he was instrumental in NOT having the hostel in the church history; he very much gave the impression he did not want the hostel next to his church. Canon Arbuthnott as the head of the Catholic Rescue Society was the only Priest in contact with the hostel, apart from Fr. Davis who was resident at the hostel.

By the way, John, the hostel was called the St. Agnes Hostel and actually accommodated about forty boys from various Catholic Homes. I trust this information is of assistance in your investigations.

Regards to you and Josie.

Colin and Eileen

Eileen and Colin,

Thank you so much for your informative email. I do everything in a hurry! I like to get my letters done in the morning before I attend to Josie's care. It's a pity I didn't get round to attempting the story of St. Agnes hostel earlier, as it is too late to be included in the book.

Eileen must have been ahead of her time asking pertinent questions about the church!

We didn't do a lot in our younger days. I am guessing that you and Eileen must have been married over 55 years ago and you are to be congratulated on staying the course. Josie and I have been married 49 years. Although I never actually stayed at the hostel I did visit fairly often to see the lads. I was "lodged" with a family in Orpington.

Best wishes to you and Eileen.

KOKO

John & Josie

Hellooooo…

I just love the way you write, John!

Some while back when inquiring about a Home in Essex I was transferred to the County Council's Archives Department where I was assured that ALL parish records were now held as well as lists of Homes of every kind. Apparently all local authorities keep such records and some go back to when records first started. I was able to name the road which was full of homes of one kind or another but still got my answer.

Just saying!! I think of you all often but feel so bogged down by ALL the personal events in Australia with regards to my family. I'm toying with the idea of going over for a while, so we'll see!

Much love to you & Josie, Caroline and Terry and anyone else wot knows me !!

Ann

Ann,

What a nice thing to say! Thank you! As they say – I gave it my best shot!

As you see I was writing to a High Churchman and was mindful that he is a well educated man. There is a saying. "It is better to be thought a fool rather than open your mouth and confirm it." I think it applies even more to writing. Your friends will make allowances but other will not. Our writings have reached a natural pause. We all did so much in the early days when our group like Topsy was growing and now we are waiting for our book (first publication). We are waiting for the book but not impatiently. Perhaps if we can keep on writing, albeit, not frenetically like before, Caroline may gather enough material to write yet another volume. We still occasionally find new members who want to tell their story. We had one earlier this year.

Terry is enjoying himself in Canada and the USA for six weeks. Caroline lives in British Columbia and he is staying with her and sorting, hopefully, some of her computer problems. Although his trip was unplanned to coincide with our book, he will be able to assist our friend Caroline with the final proof reading and possibly get to meeting the publisher Bruce Batchelor.

He had some good news when he retired from the tax man and took Caroline up on her long time invitation to stay and visit her, and also to spend a week with his older brother Max who winters in California for six months every year from his home in Nova Scotia. Caroline like most of us is not a whizz regarding under bonnet computing despite being a really good typist so hopefully Terry can give her a helping hand.

Ann, it's an awfully long way to Australia. The hours and hours for the flight alone put me off BUT of course it is different for you. Perhaps if you do go you can resolve some problems that just can't be done on Skype or Facetime. We have group members North, South, East and West of Australia and just occasionally they come over, usually to carry out some research into why they were sent out there in the first place!

In the early fifties when a group of our boys were "shipped" out there we thought it was the end! We never dreamed years later that we would see or hear from some of them again but the world is a smaller place these days and even if you aren't physically able to make the journey, modern technology opens the door to a different way to meet, see and chat to our distant friends. Whatever your decision to go or not, you know you can stay in touch and do please let us know how things are panning out.

Love,

John & Josie

ADVENTURES IN CANADA

Hi John & Josie,

I am sending this from Caroline's computer which we think is now working! Once I got past the sheer age of her PC (most of her instructions are in Latin – shorthand) and fixed a host of her problems I hope it will make life so much easier for her. I am amazed with all its faults Caroline achieves so much.

Think this confirms her tenacious appetite for getting things done; no matter the obstacles!

Bruce has sent Caroline the final manuscript to ready for printing and editing. Today we have made a start to look at it. You can be sure Caroline will not send her approval until she has checked everything! Nothing gets past her eagle eye I can assure you.

Caroline and her family are looking after me well as you can imagine and next Monday Caroline and myself are taking the ferry on a tour of the many Gulf Islands, something I am particularly looking forward to because I love being on the water. As Caroline does not have WiFi I can't send messages from her home, so I take myself off to Tim Horton's coffee shop (a chain of cafes all over Canada) where I can use their on-site WiFi that is available to all their customers. Oh, the "sacrifices" I make for our book!

Regards to you both from Caroline and myself.

KOKO

Terry

Caroline and Terry,

It sounds as though everything is fine in B.C.

I accepted and voted in favour of drawing a line and getting on with the book, but just out of interest I have sent Colin Bedford an email telling him about a part of our history that has been overlooked. I refer to the Boys Hostel in Blackheath. I had Colin look over my writing for accuracy and this has been done and now I will send it to the group.

Caroline, I hope you are making the most of Terry's expertise in dealing with computers and I know you will be looking after him while he is with you.

KOKO and love,

John & Josie

Hi John,

Good to hear from you.

Currently, I have a burst blood vessel in my right eye which happened when Terry and I were sailing through the Gulf Islands today. It is sore and prevents me from working on the proof reading for a few days; other than that all is well and good.

Very interesting to read about the Boys Hostel at Blackheath; too bad we didn't have this earlier but we needed a cut off date. Still, you and Terry will no doubt save this and the future history connected to St. Mary's for the next book!

Love to you and Josie,

Caroline

Caroline,

We were sorry to hear about your eye. It must have blighted your trip through the Gulf Islands and taken something away from your enjoyment. It must be a setback because I know what keen eyesight you have and how you enjoy spotting the wildlife, especially the eagles.

About our book. It was always going to happen with people like me coming up late with incidents in our life. But that's life and it does not stop, even when our book in finished. But let us continue collecting this social history. And as Margaret Mitchell said in her famous book, it was a way of life that is "Gone With The Wind".

We have all contributed stories and let's hope they keep coming.

Colin Bedford's email says so much about what life was like at the hostel and I will forward it to you.

All the best to you and Terry. KOKO.

John & Josie

MORE ON THE HOSTEL AND FATHER LOMAN

Hi once again, J. and J,

Further to my email regarding records of the home in Cresswell Park, they should be with the Greenwich Council. I can reveal further comments on Father Loman, who was renowned for his church collections at mass, where if he thought there was NOT enough money put in the collection tray he would send it round again AND ask for paper money only! The boys not having such riches would click the collection tray with their fingers to give the impression they had put money into the collection, and passed it on. When Eileen once went to his place, the "Palace", she commented on his lavish trappings and lifestyle that prompted her questions and, along with her friend, she was told not to attend any more! He reported Eileen and I to the head of the Hostel for courting in the grounds of the church for which I was duly fined. You will gather from this he was not a popular man and was widely viewed as a bad Ambassador of the Catholic Church. I am not usually in the business of doing character assassinations but I think it should have been brought to the attention of the Catholic Authorities at the time. His undoubted unpopularity and in general his poor relationship with the hostel AND the fact of its removal from the church history.

I trust this gives you a little more information to add to your investigation to why the Hostel was not recognized in the church history.

Regards as always to you and Josie.

Colin and Eileen

Colin and Eileen,

It was a brilliant idea from the Priest's point of view, sending the collection round again.

Eileen showed some spirit tackling Father Loman about his lifestyle. Some people find luxury barely adequate! About that fine though, perhaps you should have instructed your brief to put his wig on and let the court decide if the fine was legal. I was once rocked when in the 1950s our parish Priest Father Slocombe called out from the pulpit the maximum to be put in the plate by any working person should be 2/-. Yes, Two Shillings!

A bit of my background. When I left St. Mary's to live with the family in Orpington the Catholic Rescue Society took the view, I believe, that families taking lads should not suffer any financial loss and the advantage to the "child" would be demonstrated in other ways. When I first arrived with the family they sorted out my pay. I earned Two Pounds Ten Shillings a week from which I needed 7/6d for pocket money and 7/6d for fares. The CRS paid to make up the shortfall in my keep and pay for any clothes needed. I did think at first I was financially independent. I was proud to be paying my way and even considered doling out pocket money to the other five children who were still at school but luckily was discouraged from doing this. As soon as I learned my meagre wages were not enough to stand on my own two feet, I then secured another job with more money BUT, alas, still not enough. Anyway, Colin, I really wanted to tell you about my "church collection" in the 1950s; now I am late to pick up Josie from the "God Squad".

Always good to hear from you.

KOKO,

Josie and John

LETTER FROM MONSIGNOR NICHOLAS

Dated May 5, 2015

Dear Mr. Flynn, Thank you for your message.

I am indeed aware of the link with the Children's Society. The parish was founded as an Orphanage in 1872 when the first Priest Father William

Gowan Todd purchased what is now the presbytery for this work. Gradually the work expanded and when the Rescue Society was founded it took over the parish work. The parish hall was originally the chapel of the Orphanage. It was severely damaged during the war and restored in a new form but it is possible to find traces of the Old Chapel. The school rooms were converted into a house and is now occupied by the area Bishop. The hostel was built adjoining the presbytery and was extended in three phases. The Children's Society ceased to use the property in about 1960 and for a number of years The Vincent de Paul Society used it as a hostel. This use came to an end in 1968 and subsequently the shell of the building was adopted for offices. The church came later in 1983 and the large stained glass window at the West End shows Our Lady Queen of Heaven surrounded by children; an obvious reference to the original foundation of the parish came from this; with complaints from the neighbouring parish Priest at Greenwich who resented the establishment of a new parish. So the two things fit together. The original establishment of the Orphanage at Blackheath by Father Gowan Todd – later the foundation of the Rescue Society and the transfer of this work. You mentioned a number of Priests who served at Blackheath and were involved in the work of the hostel. I understand a clash of personalities meant relationships between the parish Priest at the time and the hostel was not always easy; particularly in the 1930s. I am very much aware of the foundation of the parish and make the care of children a special feature, not just theoretically. Part of today was spent mending the trampoline in the garden and this afternoon a visit from seven pupils from the school for instruction on Sacraments and play in the garden.

With best wishes.

Monsignor Nicholas Rothon

John,

Life at the Blackheath boys hostel had certain restrictions for the "inmates". Every boy had to be in bed by 10pm and lights out in the dormitories was at 10.30pm, except for half an hour on Tuesdays when an extension was granted on what was picture night to allow the boys to go to the cinema. A fine would have to be paid for being late in as the outside doors would be locked at 10pm and the only way in was by ringing the staff door bell. There were no restrictions on smoking, your rent for your keep was paid on Friday and what you paid was related to your earnings. Physical punishment and religious instruction was carried out by Father Davis at 9.30pm every Thursday. The hierarchy at the hostel was Mr. Cadogan, Superintendent; Ex. Guards Sergeant Major and at the Farm: Mrs. Cadogan, Matron; Ms. Carden, Cook; Fr. Davis, Resident Priest. There were also various housemen and sometimes additional help. At the age of eighteen you could no longer stay at the hostel and you were either called up for National Service OR had to find digs or somewhere else to live. I trust, John, this gives you some more insight into life at St. Agnes's Hostel at Blackheath.

As always to you, Josie and your family my fondest wishes.

Colin and Eileen

KEEP ON KEEPING ON

Terry,

It seems you were right about Caroline's "clapped out" computer. She works so hard she deserves to "treat" herself to what you and she were looking at the other day. Did you know today is V.E. Day and if we had not been given the tools to do the job we would probably be speaking in German today.

Terry, you have done a wonderful job lending your total support and encouragement with the book BUT she deserves so much better than a clapped out computer, doesn't she?

Regards,

John

Hi John and Josie,

I did suggest to Caroline that ALL "old" things should be replaced! With a glint of mischief in her eye she replied: 'Does that include *me* too?' For once I kept my mouth shut! (I know in itself how hard it may be hard for some to believe!) but do remember I bruise very easily. She is still having problems with the burst blood vessel in her eye. Needless to say this has not stopped the proof reading, just slowed it down a tad.

As a pre-birthday treat Caroline and her son-in-law Don (who is always helping Caroline out with whatever she may need) and me are going to a Pizza place noted for said Pizzas and other things on Sunday. We shall be meeting publisher Bruce and hopefully his wife too, I think in Victoria. So I am still being well looked after. I could get used to this.

KOKO

Terry McK...

Hi John,

It seems you too have an upcoming birthday very shortly as I do, so let me be the first to remind you how much older you are than me. Hope you have a nice day and get the day off from the ironing, at least!

Wish Josie a happy Mother's Day from Caroline and yours truly.

KOKO

Terry McK...

Thanks Terry and Caroline,

Michael Monaghan strolled over yesterday and we had breakfast at the local "Greasy Spoon".

KOKO.

John

WORKING WOMEN AND THEIR CHILDREN

Hi John,

I think I messed up my last email; sorry I don't know what happened, so here we go again! I hope you and your family are well. Did you notice during today's W.W. Two celebrations there was no mention of those children born out of wedlock. Their mothers in many cases worked in the factories, helping to keep the heroes moral up; and the result, Children!!

who often ended up in hardship or a children's home. Not whinging, just wondered.

Regards,

Tony Ledger

Tony,

My mother was a domestic servant and at the outbreak of war her employer rushed off to do war work, so mother had to make arrangements for me. She spent her time during the war working in the Navy, Army and Air Force Institute (NAAF) where she met her husband. After the war she returned to work for her erstwhile employer, leaving Southwark Catholic Rescue Society to look after me. You take care. KOKO.

John

Hi John,

Glad to see I am not the only one "messing" up emails then! Had a lovely day yesterday with Caroline, her daughter and Don and met Bruce Batchelor today in Victoria. Am sat sending this on a bench outside of Caroline's condo because I discovered I can connect to WiFi from there. She doesn't have it!

Because Caroline is quite rightly fussy with the final proof reading and the trouble with her eye (which is recovering well I am pleased to say) I fear Bruce may not get it back before I depart these shores for home, which is not what I was hoping, but I know Caroline will do her hardest to make it happen. Oh well, that's life I suppose.

Say Hi to Josie and have a really happy birthday next Sunday the 17th.

KOKO

Terry McK…

Hi John,

So true! My mother worked in a munitions factory. Brother Keith was born in 1943. His father was a Canadian. We eventually made our way across the ocean to Canada in 1949. My mother married to a Canadian and life began again here. I was working at twelve and my younger brother went into the Air Force as soon as he was able. He spent time with the U.S. Marines for a while in Vietnam, then on to a guard at a Penitentiary. At fifteen I started life as a printer, leaving the trade to retire aged seventy. As we all did. We Kept On Keeping On.

Regards to all.

Daniels

Roy,

You have said a great deal using very few words. Working from the age of twelve! For goodness sake! I thought we had it tough. And then not retiring until aged seventy! You mention your younger brother – a hero. Was the whole thing to do with leaving your parents home. Vietnam was a terrible war! Thankfully Harold Wilson kept us out of that one. Roy, I am reading a book by Christopher Hitchens "The Trial of Henry Kissinger" and one of the facts included in the book was that the war in Vietnam could have ended in 1968, when at a peace conference in Paris, Nixon persuaded South Vietnam politicians to hold out as they would get a better deal from a Nixon administration. Nixon was the new president and the war went on for another four years and an extra 20,000 American lives were lost. The final peace agreement was similar to what was on the table in 1968.

KOKO.

John

FIRST *CONTACT* NEWS LETTER (DECEMBER 1954) TO THE BOYS FROM THE BLETCHINGLY TRAINING FARM

Once the boys reached the age of fifteen, the work place beckoned. In the case of St. Mary's, Gravesend, and St. Joseph's, Orpington, unless they had parents, they were given the chance of working on a Training Farm in Bletchingly, Surrey or going to St. Agnes Hostel at Blackheath in London. Colin Bedford is the nearest we have to an expert on the Agnes Hostel. No official news or circulars were issued from this place which is / was a shame, since in the fifties the lads had to do their National Service which involved at least two years in the military. Most of what we know about the hostel has been supplied from Colin.

I have passed information supplied by him to the members.

They (the boys from The Farm) seemed to have a great social life. The lads at Blackheath may have had a great time but there is no record of the activities. Now, contrast this with the farm! From December 1954 news sheets grandly titled *CONTACT* were sent to the lads doing their National Service around the world. I have these sheets thanks to Joe Gannon, who had kept and sent them to me when he first became ill and shortly afterwards passed away.

Below is the first *CONTACT* – the next *CONTACT* is dated February 1955 and I shall endeavour to type these newsletters word for word rather then vetting or editing it. I have made a mistake of assuming if I don't know a name, neither will any of you. Please bear with me and ignore any information you consider boring. And, off we go!

— Delvin John Flynn

CONTACT NEWS LETTER

In the *First Edition,* mention is made of Jack Norman, Jimmy McGuinness, Terry Graham and Laurie Wyse; they are all on page one.

Page two. Pte. Alan Burgess who was with the RAMC at the Royal Herbert Hospital in Woolwich. Terry Graham, John O'Brien and Paddy Daly were shown working at Rowfold Estate, Billinghurst, Sussex. Tony (now known as Jim) was working at Old Swains Farm, Leigh near Reigate, and said by Mr. Dill to be doing well. Jimmy Florio has a good job at Southbourne Court, Southwester near Horsham. Pte. Jack Norman was stationed at Aldershot. John Dunlop is working and living in Caterham, Surrey, and was still living there when we saw him a few years ago. Pat Brody didn't care for the country life and is living in Streatham, SW16. Mr. Loveman is busy sending his flowers to market. He is being helped or hindered by Ron Graham and Joe Powell (we are still in touch with Joe).

We played Dartford at football and got licked seven-zero. I do not think we should enter for the World Cup!

COUNT OUR BLESSINGS
We have nineteen boys here just now and I bet it is the first time they have been called a blessing!

NO ROOM AT THE INN
Will those who want to stay over Christmas let us know very soon or you may find we are full up. And we should hate to disappoint you.

DANCING TIME
The boys had a great time at the Bligh's Hotel with a warm welcome from Fr. O'Sullivan and the members of the Sevenoaks Catholic Club and they are returning the compliment by inviting them to an evening early in the New Year.

WHOOPS A DAISY
A jolly good evening was had at the Streatham Ice Rink. Some sad news to follow re: Alan Burgess.

NAMES UNFAMILIAR TO ME, also mentioned in The News Letter:

John Lynch	Bob Bryant
Raymond Legge	Frank Dennis
Bill Turner	Michael Sheridan
George Brown	Laurie Wyse
Fred Clayton (passed on)	Bill Burns
Dan Dooley	

Mr. Donald (the cowman) has left and Mr. Ketley has taken over in charge of the cows. Mr. Ketley takes the boys for games twice a week in the library.

GOING OFF WITH A BANG
Friends came from Bermondsey and had lots of fun and dancing but alas a spark set off ALL the fireworks in one go. There is a request for a letter from Joe Gannon and Derek Aylett. This year the hope is that someone else will do it. We have marked the Marian Year by a grotto of Our Lady. This was built by Alan Burgess and is just outside the chapel.

END OF THE BEGINNING
This brings us to a close at the end of our first effort. We hope you like it and will help us to fill it by sending your news, which will enable us all to keep in *CONTACT*.

END

(Posted to the KOKO group by (Delvin) John Flynn on May 13, 2015)

Hello John,

Thanks for posting this news letter on. I find it fascinating as it brings back so many memories, particularly the names of those I had long forgotten. We hope you and Josie are well.

Best Wishes.

Pat & Mavis

AUSTRALIA

Mavis,

Thank you. Ask Paddy if he know what happened to Derek Harwood. It was customary when we went to Dymchurch once a year for our holidays that the two eldest boys travelled with Father Baker. In 1954 the role fell to D.H. and me. D.H. subsequently disappeared and I never heard from him again.

Keep looking on *CONTACT*. There will be other interesting names and places mentioned. It is time-consuming work but I believe others like P. will derive pleasure from reading *CONTACT*. We were so much younger then!

KOKO.

John & Josie

THE ARMY AND YOU

BY LESLIE HAYES
DATED MAY 18, 2015

Every man at the age of eighteen has to serve two years in the Armed Forces unless he is an apprentice or studying at University. Some look on these two years as a waste of time but if you looked at it as a chance to prepare yourself for a return to civilian life it is not true. One has to think for yourself and not just follow the crowd. This applies in or out of the Army. The type of company is up to each individual. There are good companions and there are bad; it is your own choice. You can lie on your bed or go to the NAAFI. On the other hand you can take up the facilities offered in the way of Night Classes. If you use some of your spare time to learn while in the Forces there is less risk of unemployment when you come out. The majority of men do not think you odd if you practice religion. Be sincere about it and do not preach to the others and they will respect your principles. I find most Servicemen are good fellows and good friends. The idle and immoral ones are in the minority.

CONTACT #2, FEBRUARY 1955

As transcribed and posted by John Flynn

HOME NEWS BY THE EDITOR

It seems strange to be talking of Christmas just as we are looking for signs of Spring but this is our first meeting before then. The holiday was well spent here in the usual way. The house was pretty full with the addition of our visitors who we are always pleased to welcome. It was quite a military affair. It seemed that one was forever meeting soldiers on the stairs or round the place.

On Boxing Day a party of us went to the Grand Theatre at Croydon for a pantomime. It was the usual thing. All pantomimes run to the same pattern. One wonders why they are given different names! This was "Babes in the Woods" and it was exactly the same as "Aladdin" any other year. Still, it is part of the Christmas routine and anyway who wants to be sensible at Christmas?

The snow came some weeks ago and I expect most of you can remember just how it looks here. Stats. Hill proved to be the downfall of all traffic. Fortunately we always have South Park to save us from being completely cut off. It was very cosy to sit round the log fire and see the snow falling. In spite of the snow and cold the longer evenings tell us Spring will not be long now. This is a busy time and especially this year as it hoped to have an Open Day in June and needs the gardens to be gay and colourful; you well know that means hard work.

In the last issue Father told you about the Open Day and we hope to see many old friends for the occasion.

Mr. Loverman thinks we will never do it, what with the boilers flooding the fire and making it go out and the boys driving him up the wall. He reckons he will be up the creek before June and stone bonkers (in Cockney slang). Mr. Carr who assists in the house takes some of the boys for basket work. Some of these boys show quite a talent for flower pot holders and table mats. We are also making plaster casts and frames which we hope to flog to an unsuspecting public! We don't intend to give them any mercy.

We have a new boy called Michael Feeney. He will not be known to any of you as he comes from Kingston on Hull, Yorkshire. This month we lost Peter Hughes. He came to us from Sunderland and returned North, having finished his training. So you can see we are getting well known all over the country.

CONTACT – PAGE 4

Here is one address you have not had: 23212341 Fus. Maher M., Royal Fusiliers H.M. Tower of London, EC3. We had a visit from this very smart soldier at Christmas but not since. We would still like to hear from Bill Burns. If any of you know his address you might let us have it. Father says he got a Christmas card from Ronald Beddice in Canada but gave no address.

Mr. McDonnell the tractor drive has left and we have a new one starting soon.

OUR PORTRAIT GALLERY

We would like more pictures of the old boys to put around the house. We could make a competition of it with a prize of a bag of Palm toffees for the most handsome face. So we would very much appreciate your photograph, postcard size if you think your face is worth it! We can stand it.

GIVING IT A NAME
Although we started off by calling this news circular CONTACT we were not quite sure whether it would be suitable. If any of you can suggest one which you consider more suitable we would be glad to have your idea. Michael Sheridan has arrived from his leave. He says he has about fourteen months to go before his demob and does not intend to make the Army his career.

GETTING TOGETHER
We are keen to have a reunion day for all our old boys some time in the summer. The Open Day we hope to have had would hardly be suitable as we would have so many other people here (we hope). It is thought that July would be a good month. Could you help us by giving some ideas of a date you could manage? If we could get a line on this we could fix a date and go ahead with some preparations. We want to make it a really good affair and would love to have some clues as to the number expected. Do keep writing to us to give us a chance to make it a good "Do".

J. Dill says thank you very much for your letter, Paul. We are all very pleased that you have "passed out". When we see you next we will be looking for your wings.

Come and see us soon.

To Alan Burgess of the Linseed Lancers. Thanks for your letter too. I trust you have not killed too many sick rookies with your nursing. What about a visit from you?

To Dennis Conway. Thank you for your letter. The raincoat you brought back from Kingston is apparently Tony Fowler's and the one you left there is Ken Marchant's.

Tony Sheasby is going into hospital for treatment for an ulcer.

To Laurie Wyse. I hope you got your Pay Draft from the Exeter Pay Office. Although it is not much it will help to buy your cigs. for a few days.

To Mick Maher. When you telephone again try to make it before 11pm. After all us old people cannot burn the candle at both ends like you youngsters!
To you all – Matron and I send our best wishes for your future. We are always glad to see you and hear from you. God Bless.

More to come !!
Signed: Paul – Paul Norman

KOKO GROUP EMAILS, *cont'd*

ANTICIPATING THE BOOK LAUNCH

To: John Murray

Hi John,

It was really good to speak to you and see you eventually! My fault, I think. As I said I had a lovely time in Sidney, B.C. and Caroline looked after me regally.

I hope the PDF file of the book arrived in tact. Really enjoyed your story along with all the rest of them and the photos too. As said I will contact those who will receive a copy from me when I finally get my hands on them. I'm thinking possibly end of July/August.

John I know will be delighted to meet both you and your wife whenever we can arrange it. I will be seeing him and Josie in a couple of weeks. Always a warm welcome at Chez Flynn.

Congratulations on winning FA cup final tickets and I hope you have a great day or two. Not jealous at all, me!! Hope your son makes a good recovery. The enclosed photo is John Flynn and left to right Teresa Downy (of Cabrini), Caroline Whitehead and Josie. This was taken when Caroline visited us in 2013 and was in Orpington.

Regards to you and all your family.

KOKO.

Terry McK...

Caroline,

You really must take care of yourself. I know it is difficult working on a computer that you are not used to. I thought at first to congratulate you on getting a new machine but when I read on further I realised this was not the case. We are all waiting patiently for the book but again you must not worry about keeping us waiting. We want you to stay alive and well and not be "dead on time" with the book.

KOKO and best wishes

Josie and John

John,

Delighted to hear you are impressed with the cover of the book and hope when you read its contents and the emails going back and forth over the years from our members, it will tell the reader how tenacious we are to keep on keeping on our KOKO alive.

A message from the publisher to you: Amazon's database does not allow the paperback to have only an editor and not an author so I am listed as the author. With Kindle this condition is not required. I have asked Bruce for the name of the reporter of the Gravesend newspaper and once I receive it I will forward to you.

It was great speaking to you and Josie. I never quite know when to ring you as I am not sure of the time when you have your evening meal. If my timing was inconvenient do please let me know. The books should arrive within two weeks at which time I will airmail you a copy. The rest will go to those members who generously contributed towards the cost of OUR publication. This was greatly appreciated. Irena at Cabrini will also have a copy. The belated birthday card with enclosure was given to Terry. I hope it won't be long before it reaches you.

With Chris's news of emigrating to France does that mean you and Josie will visit soon? Once again, John, it was my pleasure and an honour to ensure your years of hard work in keeping our group members updated of current and historical events, and for them to be able to tell their own stories in "The Boys of St. Mary's" to keep their history alive for generations to come.

Take care.

Love and hugs to you and Josie.

Caroline

Letter to Polly Toynbee: Author, Journalist

Dated May 31, 2015

Dear Polly Toynbee,

You called at my home over thirty years ago and my story was included in your book "Lost Children". Since that time I formed a writing group. The members all had stayed or had associations with Children's Home. Our oldest member is almost 89 years old.

You may just cast your eye over the book which is available from Amazon titled "The Boys of St. Mary's" and may be able to give it – I think you call it a plug. I know what a busy lady you are and I regularly read your daily newspaper column and you must be fed up with me contacting you every thirty years.

Signed:

John Flynn OR Tom O'Mara in your book...

Caroline,

Below is a note from the well known journalist Polly Tonybee.

John

Dear John,

Many thanks. I will read it with pleasure.

Hope you are well.

Polly

Ann,

Let me write later!

You are so funny!

KOKO,

Love,

Josie and John

WOW... WOW... WOW!!

It's happening then or rather has happened. Many congratulations to you ALL for achieving this book, John. I am so looking forward to reading it as will so many Gravesenders. Some months ago I offered to put it on Facebook but didn't want to "muscle" in on your project... or is it likely that Caroline will do this when contact is made with the Gravesend reporter? I'll wait and see what you think. I haven't written to Caroline for months but do receive your news regularly which is so appreciated.

This little gang of yours has quite touched my heart and I feel I have known you all for ages.

Thank you for including me in your Group!

Much love to you all,

Ann... xx

"Announcement" on Facebook

A teeny bit of "crawling" but I really did have to tell them; because of that I gleaned myself about St. Mary's as well as the group.

Many of you were interested in the forthcoming book about St. Mary's Orphanage in Gravesend. The GTN Committee has given me permission to let you know on this site, the book has now been published and is available in paperback and on Kindle. The details are as follows:

"The Boys of St. Mary's"... paperback ISBN 978-1-927755-23-5 and Kindle 978-1927755-24-2.

Many of the photographs were seen on this site which meant so much to the past residents of St. Mary's as they had of their own to share.

They have me to thank you ALL for your contributions.

Ann   Dated June 5, 2015

'morning, Ann,

What can I say? But excellent news of your behalf to give much-needed publicity to our group of members, whose stories and emails in the book of "The Boys of St. Mary's" need to be told to children in the schools and libraries about history of past events we hope never to return. Your insight to put the book on Facebook and the feedback is encouraging. As John M. Murray once said: "It would make a good film", not only to have the audience laughing at the antics of the young lads but also in tears.

Six books were sold instantly on Ebooks within minutes of the release mid-Friday last. I am hoping that John's connection with Polly Tonybee, journalist, along with the Gravesend newspaper, she may give us the exposure we need. I feel sure the book will be a success bearing in mind with today's literature, none could match the dialogue of communication which continues within our writers group!

The final chapter in the book relating to OUR records was extensive and when reading its contents you will gather the communication between John, Terry and Cabrini/Diagrama to obtain satisfaction (tongue in cheek) our files be protected. Will watch this space as advised by Terry!

I am sure John is so pleased now the book is published and with the encouraging reports of interest shown at this early stage of its release.

Sincere thanks, Ann. You always come through, even at critical times to yourself.

With love and KOKO

Caroline

Good morning!

I think the day has started well. Last night I sought permission from Roger Simmons on FB's Gravesend Then and Now to announce the publication of "The Boys of St. Mary's". Advertising on these sites is no longer allowed. However I messaged Roger first who discussed it with other committee members and they agreed I could "announce" its availability!! In the first five minutes of having mentioned it on FB we had eleven "likes". One purchase and an excellent comment. Another has put an Amazon feature of the book on the site. So… watch this space!

On a different note I seem to have lost track somewhere along the way the outcome of John and Terry's meeting with Cabrini and Diagrama. Have they assured you of the safety of ALL your personal records and access to them??

Much love to y'all and best wishes for every success with sales for the book.

KOKO

Ann

John,

I have been silent for some time because I have been involved in other matters. All those matters have now come to an end and therefore I have ordered the book from Amazon and am looking forward to reading it.

John O'Donnell

John,

I'm thoroughly enjoying the Ebook. I have correspondence from John Michael Murray in the distant past lives (lives in Cardiff, nicht whar?) and would love to contact him having read his piece (Laundry Boy) in the book – some amazing similarities. I have both a John Murray and a Michael Murray in my address book. If you feel it appropriate please forward this missive to the right Mr. M. for him to contact me if he feels so fit.

Many many thanks and to you Caroline – a winner!

Glen Cawdeary

Glen,

It was a dare but as Del Boy says, "He who dares wins".

So glad you are enjoying Caroline's skillful art of managing so many stories and emails in one book. Let's hope for her sake the sales rocket.

Look after yourself, Glen.

KOKO

John Flynn

Hello Glen,

I hope you do not mind me contacting you. I read with great interest your email your time at St. Mary's. Much of what you say I can relate to, having spent ten years in the care of The Sisters of Mercy and The Sisters of Charity. (Both are so wrongly named!) Like you I arrived at St. M's aged seven in 1950 having spent four years in an Orphanage in Brighton called St. Anne's. The Mother Superior had me moved as it was a girls orphanage. She must have thought their "Chastity" was under threat! So to St. M's I went. I suffered the humiliation meted out to bed-wetters many times. I felt the full force of the hairbrush or a Nun's hand and occasionally Father Baker's boot. We must have passed in the doorway as I left in December 1956 to go home to live with my mother. I am retired living in Cardiff. I am trying to put together my memories of those times, particularly working the laundry under Sister Brendan. Hope to send them to Caroline for a joint publication.

Do keep sending in your memories.

John Michael Murray

John,

I managed to find your missive above in my archives. Have just read your piece in the book – lots of parallel memories of names in common. Would love to meet up – we're not that far from you over the border. Other John (F) you can see that my digging through old emails (once a hoarder) obviates any action on your part which I'm sure you would have initiated your usual expediency. YES, I do use expressions like that – I remember "The Good Old Days".

Glen

John (O'Donnell)

Caroline is encouraged by the response to the book as, along with great help from Terry, she has spent many hours bringing the whole project to fruition. I hope you enjoy the book, especially as you not only stayed at St. Mary's but have taken an interest over many years in matters relating to children and of course written some emails too. I agree with your sentiments regarding trying to support your local bookshop BUT in this case outlets to sell the book, which we must remember was published at Caroline's personal expense, along with some donations from some of our members, as limited.

KOKO

Josie and John.

Dear John,

I know of no kinder person than yourself, despite having travelled many journeys. Your accolades are indeed appreciated but as you know with the book of St. Mary's, it was an honour and privilege to be sent on this journey in the first place and given the opportunity of publishing stories of the "Old Boys" during the good and bad times of the 1920s plus era. That we are able to record our history for all time, without the consensus of being too judgmental to the then caregivers who to all intents and purposes, did what they could with the best material available to them, will remain.

Mavis Heffernan in Victoria, Australia has promised to catalogue the book. Also it is hoped to arrange delivery to Sue Stafford in Freemantle, Western Australia and the "Old Boys" organization in Perth.

To John O'D, I am delighted you continue to take an ongoing interest in the welfare of children and also with the history of St. Mary's. Had my late brother William (Bill) been alive today he would have been "chuffed". His photograph at Bletchingly Farm is in the book.

KOKO.

Take care.

Caroline

Clare and Patrick,

A book has been published about St. Mary's and can be obtained on Amazon. The author is one of our members – Caroline Whitehead.

Regards.

(Delvin) John Flynn.

John,

Thank you for forwarding your message to Alfred Cooke. Is he a member of the Group?

KOKO

Caroline

Caroline,

Alfred Cooke AKA Patrick Slevin. Patrick learned of his father and after many years decided to take his father's name. He is a bit of a character but sadly does not put pen to paper very often.

He sent me a card for my birthday but apart from that has not been in touch for years. However emails regarding our writings were sent to him using his original name.

KOKO

Josie and John

Ann,

Pretty amazing! Caroline is justifiably pleased with the response after so much work on a clapped out computer. When Terry visited her he was astounded by her whole approach to writing with, in many many instances emails that were re-typed rather than copied, cut and pasted.

Ann, you must take a bow too for making use of Facebook!

So let's KOKO

Love Josie and John

From a person named Michael (not sure which one)

As a former resident of Gravesend I found this book to be a thoroughly compelling read from a group of writers who were all institutionalized as children and continue to be under the church control and authorities throughout their life to this current day. Their stories as children and their emails with each other highlight the skulduggery, lies and deceit of the authorities which led to their pains!

Anguish and frustration that continue to exist are somewhat unbelievable.

Well done to All the writers concerned; it opened my eyes and I thank you.

Michael

(Undated)

CONTACT #3, JUNE 1955

As I mentioned previously some of the boys at the age of 15 years went to the Hostel at Blackheath. Some went to the Training Farm at Bletchingly and others, like me, went to live with families.

Joe Gannon, an amazing chap who was liked by everyone, was a bit of a hoarder, and just before he died twenty-four years ago in the USA he sent me his bits and pieces which keep turning up in my crodge (personal effects). Among the bits and pieces were news sheets sent out from the Farm to the boys serving in the Armed Services in many parts of the world. These news sheets were lovingly tapped out on a very old fashioned typewriter which must have taken an inordinately long time to do.

I know because I am not a super dooper typist like Caroline.

Hopefully many of our group will see their names included but unfortunately the Hostel at Blackheath didn't have a similar scheme to help keep the boys in touch with one another.
— *(Delvin) John F...*

PAGE 1
Being the odds and ends of interest to our old boys of St. Mary's Farm, this Issue has been promised for some time and a few of you have been asking when it was coming. The days have been rather full here lately and that is the excuse for being late. It is not a very good excuse but is as good as any I heard from some of you lot when late for meals! Now I can get up off my knees.

THE MORE WE ARE TOGETHER THE HAPPIER WE WILL BE
So runs the words of a very old song. We thought we would try it out

and invited quite a few of the boys to a reunion at Easter. About twenty of them turned up and a happy time we all spent. Easter Sunday we sat down to a very nice lunch presided over by Father. Mike Sheridan made a speech on behalf of the visitors. It wasn't the speech he had prepared, and he had to make one up. It was quite a success. Well done, Sherry! We shall see you as an MP and I don't mean a Redcap (military police).

The football match was really something. It was Sheridan Swifts V Johnsons Juveniles. The enthusiasm was terrific! On another page you can read a professional report of the match by our Sports Reporter who we let off the chain for the occasion. We also had a sung High Mass for which some of the visitors lent us their voices in the loft. Most of them left us late on Easter Monday and it was agreed by all that it had been a happy occasion for everyone and it was grand to see so many of the "family" together.

ASKING FOR MORE
Like Oliver Twist, we wanted more! The Easter get together was so successful that we repeated the invitation for Whitsun. Of course we did not get quite as many but a very pleasant holiday was spent by us all. We have learned by these two efforts that a reunion is a good thing and is worth all the extra work involved. We are busy now trying to think up another reason to get the "family" together again.

Any suggestions?

BULLING UP
As most of you know by now the farm is celebrating its 21st birthday. The occasion being marked by an Open Day on the 18 June. Quite a few people are expected, subject to the Rail Strike being over. His Lordship the Bishop will be here and also The Earl of Munster to join this happy family day. Some of the boys are hoping to join in with us. You can be sure that our thoughts will be with so many of you on this day, as they are most evenings at family Rosary, when we say a dedication for ALL our old boys. The house has been repainted and also the boys sitting room. The place is more like Butlins every week!

COME INTO THE GARDEN MAUDE

This is the title of a very old ballad long before your time, but if you care to come into the garden you will be glad. Mr. Loverman has worked very hard, helped by his boys to get the flower beds planted.

Given enough time they should look a lovely sight. He has also had a very successful cucumber season.

PAGE TWO
WHERE IS HE?

Perhaps you will find some answers here. These are the addresses we have.

- 23225365 Trpr. Hughes T.R. MT Troop. HQ Squadron. 8th TRT BOAR 16.
- 22562151 Sig. M Sheridan. 4 Con Troop, 1 Sqdn.11 Air Formation. Sig. Regt. BOAR 15.
- 23219266 Sig. Conway D. 1 Line Distribution Troop. 1 Sqdn. 18th Army Group. Sig. Regt. BOAR 4.
- 23097570 Gnr. W. Officers Mess. 10th Field Regt. RA. BOAR 15.
- 23237839 Sig. Daly. P.5 Regt. Sqdn. 1 Gallow Gate Camp. Richmond. Yorkshire.
- J. Floria P/J Mess H 162. HMS OCEAN. GPO, LONDON.
- 22569120 Sig. Hayes. B Troop. B Sqdn. 1 Corps. Sig. Regt. BOAR 15.
- 4084782 Cpl. Johnson. J.W. GCT Section. No.11 S of RA. RAF Hedsnesford. Staffs.
- 23212341 Fus. Maher. Royal Fusiliers. D Coy. Connaught Bks. Dover, Kent.
- 22756241 Dvr. C. Neil. D. Pltn. 102 Coy. RASC. 6th Armoured Div. BOAR 12.
- 23213670 Pte. Norman No 6 Platoon. B. Coy. Corruna Bks. Para. Regt. Waddon, East Croydon.
- D. Aylett. 9 Merebank Lane. Waddon, East Croydon.
- F. Dennis, 21 The Square, Leigh, Tonbridge, Kent.
- T. Mills, Brasted Place Farm, Brasted near Sevenoaks, Kent.

- Terry and Ronnie Graham are both at Rowlands Estate, Billinghurst, Sussex.
- Chris Stewart, Heatherview Nurseries.
- Javis Brookj. Crowborough, Sussex.
- Malcolm Bedford, 4 Beaufort Road, Kingston on Thames, Surrey.

We hope there is at least one address you wanted from the above list. Jimmy McGuinness we think is in the Forces somewhere. He has not let us know. If anyone has his address we would be glad to have it. Paul Norman is now a paratrooper, having completed his jumps. He has paid us several visits and looks very smart. Mike Sheridan spent his very long leave with us and was a great help to Mr. Loverman. Pat Heffernan who went from here to Blackheath is now in the Royal Navy. We do not have his new address yet. All the boys listed have visited us in the last few weeks. In fact there is hardly a week when one of the boys is not visiting. John Coles is staying with us for a few weeks and hopes to go into the Navy shortly. Dennis Conway writes from Germany: 'The cigarettes and beer are cheap'. Don't spend too much on either, Con.

The addresses you asked for are here.

To Bill Burns: It was a nice surprise to hear from you. Sorry I was long in writing back. I mislaid your address.

To Terry Hughes: Another pleasant surprise to hear from you too. I really thought you had forgotten us. I like to remember and believe me we do NOT forget any of you.

PAGE THREE
PAINTING THE CLOUDS WITH SUNSHINE
We did not get as far as that! But having brought some Lloyd Loom chairs, Jimmy Florio set about painting them. He did them in three different colours, assisted by Joe Power. It has certainly brightened up the sitting room. Jimmy will be pleased to hear that his flower basket from the ceiling is doing just fine. Plenty of geraniums in bloom now. And the chairs are how you left them; no painting out.

To Johnnie Johnson: many thanks for the report included in this issue. You appeared to be having a good time at the Whitsun dance. If I

THE COURAGE TO LOOK BACK 45

had known you needed the stairs for a long period I could have provided cushions! After all we did provide soft lights and semi sweet music. Keep us informed of "developments"! We think it is ever such jolly hockey sticks. It must be simply wonderful for you. "Gertcha"!

To Paddy Daly: don't try to tell me you are still busy "bulling up". Your letter was very welcome. But I hope your first is not your last.

Tony Sayers has gone into the Armoured Corps. He has not written yet.

Many thanks for your letter, Sherry. I will answer it in a day or two. Glad you like your new posting.

John Lynch was down at Whitsun. He tell me he went to Rome and saw the Pope. We hope to include an article from him in this issue. Thanks John.

Chris Stewart was another visitor at Whitsun. It has been a long time since he came. I hope you will not wait so long for your next visit.

Another to visit was Malcolm Bedford, roaring up the drive on his motorbike. Take it easy, Malcolm, or you may come off before you are ready. There was so much response for photographs. You see when you talk about the old boys, we can't say 'you know, the good looking one', because you are all so good looking! We would like your picture to remind us. The prize bag of aniseed balls for the most handsome is still unclaimed.

More painting: The firm of Burgess and McCarthy Unlimited are painting the chapel and a good job they are making of it.

Tony Welsh and Joe Keegan are two who have left in recent weeks for outside jobs.

Alan Burgess, having no further use for the Army, has returned here and hopes to be going to a job shortly.

Vincent McCarthy came to us from Blackheath. He thinks he prefers life in the country

ADDITIONS TO THE FAMILY
Among the recent arrivals we have Derek Harwood from Gravesend. Peter Collins from Orpington. Gerald Ellwand from Durham. Roy Carter from Canterbury and Joe Irvine from Edinburgh. We haven't had one

from the West Indies yet! But knowing Father we cannot be too sure of that!

To Les Hayes: it is about time we had a letter from you. We have not heard from you for months. I hope synonyms have not got to you!

GETTING ALL PUFFED UP
Derek Aylett is undergoing training at Croydon for Glass Blowing. He likes is very much. I suppose it is better than froth blowing! To read the letters you send makes us at home to be very dull. Just listen to a few extracts... Dennis Conway is in Essen. He says he is going on a scheme in which they will cover 300 miles across Germany up to the frontier of Belgium. Sherry says he has travelled across Germany to Holland and Belgium. Jimmy Florio sails to Bristol, Liverpool and on to Hamburg and probably Denmark, then on to Norway. When we all get together again we will be sitting up all night listening to your yarns and experiences. I think some of you could spend an hour writing an interesting article for "CONTACT". Life here is dull in comparison. What goes on here. Well you know it all. We have a daybreak and nightfall. This is a pretty regular thing here and does not excite us any more. A boy lifts some of Mr. Loverman's tomatoes. The cows get loose and waltz all over the Chrysanths and the "cow blokes" are late getting to the sheds every other morning. So on your travels; just give your eyes a chance and try to remember to write to us stay-at-home folks.

PAGE FOUR
What a game of football! There was bags of enthusiasm for this match; I must say until the day of the match itself, when four characters found excuses not to play. And so with nine a side the battle commenced. My team were all over our opponents for the first few minutes, then we simply collapsed. Sheridan's Swifts took advantage of our disorganized side and sent many a fatal ball past Goalie Georgie Brown just as he slipped down to the village to get an ice cream. The score at half time was 4-0 down. Although my team fought against overwhelming odds, we just could not get the ball into the net. It was due to Jimmy Florio's defence tactics of bull-like-charges to scare the living daylights out of my team.

Joe Power and Johnny O'Brien did some fine work for Johnson's Wanderers and between them scored our one and only goal. Star of the match was without doubt Jackie Norman. He must have been in every place all at once. So much physical training back at camp. Mike Sheridan proved his qualities as captain and kept his team together. He had to do a bit of shouting to achieve this. His long legs helped him score many a goal. In the second half my team were just about all in; so were the others come to that only ours was far more noticeable. Knocker showed off his laziness saying, 'I don't want to play. I am fed up.' What a man! So three more goals were scored against us. The referee, Alan Burgess, must have blown his heart out having so many centres. The game ended 9-1 to Sheridan's Swifts and so came an exchange of cheers. Three in all.

Many thanks to the referee for his handling of the game. His decision was final and thanks again to all who played for being such good sports. By the way where Jimmy Florio's name was mentioned insert Dennis Conway. Jimmy was in our team. I would like through the medium of "CONTACT" to send out to all the old boys of St. Mary's farm whether known or unknown, sincere best wishes and good luck in all they do. And thanks to those who stayed over for Easter for helping to make the holiday a howling success. I really enjoyed every moment of it.

John goes on to mention all the staff and on behalf of them I accept your thanks and good wishes. As I have said elsewhere in this issue the extra work is really worthwhile when we see you all together and enjoying yourselves.

FROM FATHER
John Kelly, 6 Evington Road, Leicester.
I am near the end of my course of motor engineering and hope to be in a job soon after Whitsun. I have every faith that I shall always remember you and the staff at the Farm. Please remember me to them and all the boys.

John McNeil writes: I am very pleased indeed to receive your letter. It makes Army life more cheerful. We have fish four times a day. It's cooked differently each time. We have fish cakes, fried fish, boiled fish and burnt fish. I have grown two fins and a tail.

Best wishes to the lads.

Bill Burns writes: Sorry I will not be able to come to the Reunion. I have been in the Army since January. I am doing driving and Batman for my Commanding Officer. How is the Farm? I did well at my job at Elm Farm. My boss wants me to come back when I have finished with the Army.

22847358 Sig. Lynch J. Barrack Room, 100 Block. No.1 Wireless Regt. R. Signals BOAR 12 , writes: Early next year I hope to take P.H.S. in Botany. Every spare moment I am delving into books. I hear you heard from my old friend Ronald Beddice. I would appreciate his address: 41 West Lake Crescent, Toronto, Ontario, Canada.

Munster is quite an historical place and is the Catholic capital of Germany. Although heavily bombed it has been restored to its former beauty. You would admire the Prince Bishop Palace. Magnificent in its structure with botanical gardens. I am a member of one or two societies run by the students.

The Anglo German Dramatic Group put on "Hay Fever" and "The Man With A Load of Mischief".

Kind regards to all the staff and boys. With an eye for the future make the most of your life at the Farm. If you let trifles bother you then you will be grumbling through life.

[Since this was written John has been to Rome and hopes to go to Spain.]

CONTACT #4, AUGUST 1955

ALAN BURGESS – R.I.P.

It is with deep sorrow to report the sudden and most unexpected death of Alan by drowning on 1st August when bathing in Balcombe Lake with a party of our boys. Alan swam out of his depth and when seized by cramp James Florio and Jack Norman swam to his rescue but were unable to save him despite their desperate and brave attempts. The Requiem Mass took place on Friday after Alan's body laid in repose through the night. At the inquest the Coroner returned a verdict of death by misadventure and paid tribute to those who had gone to his rescue and to the scouts who gave artificial respiration for over two and a half hours. Naturally Alan's death caused great sorrow in the house. Alan was loved and admired by us all for his fearless and straightforward character. He was proud of his faith and would not hesitate to say where he stood if anything were proposed against faith or decency.

I am sure all the old boys will remember him in their prayers and to his Aunt Miss Berkley, present, with a large concourse at his funeral, we extend our deepest sympathy.

R.I.P.

FROM OUR MAIL BAG

779 Sigm. McGinty R. C1 Troop Sqdrn. 1 Corps. R.Signals Regt. BOAR 15 – writes:

I think it is about time I dropped you a line to let you know how I am. Well, I'm doing fine, I am now enjoying the sun in Germany. It's a lot different from Malta and I think I prefer this country because it looks more like Blighty.

Sigm. Sheridan. M. Con Troop 1 Sqdrn. 11 Air Formation. Sig. Regt. BOAR 15 – writes:
We have finished NATO exercise and are collecting cable stores left behind. I am writing this before I start a course for promotion. If I pass this and another course before Christmas I will become a full Corporal. I have met a very nice fellow who lives near Redhill Hospital. I went to Mass on Sunday at the local village. It was very long. There was a procession in the evening.

I read about the Farm's coming of age in *The Sunday Mirror*.

ODDS AND ENDS OF INTEREST TO THE MEMBERS OF OUR FAMILY AT HOME AND AWAY FROM FATHER ARBUTHNOTT
I am sure you are all shocked as we were by the sad loss of Alan Burgess. We were quite heart broken that terrible night. I suppose it wakes us all up to the fact of death and brings it suddenly nearer to us all. The prayers said at the graveside remind us to think we will surely follow. There is no sense in trying to ignore this. Alan with all his faults never forgot the purpose of his life to serve God. He will do much for us in Heaven and we cannot think we have separated from him really.

The lovely warm weather has made the Farm a beautiful place and I can hear the sound of the reaper as I write this. Yesterday we went to a party in Brighton. Enjoy the good weather and I hope you are happy at the moment, boys.

God Bless you.

Father

Father Young, whom many of you know, has made a film of the Farm in colour. It was taken in the early Spring and is really lovely. Some of the boys we discovered had real film star profiles. We have not told them this or we should have had to had it done in Cinemascope to fit their heads in! We hope to show it to some of you when you come home.

GROWING UP
As we told you in our last edition, we celebrated the 21st Birthday at the Farm on 18th June. We had over 600 visitors. The Bishop welcomed all

the visitors and made a very happy speech as did the Earl of Munster. You would have blushed to hear the nice things said about our boys past and present.

LET'S HAVE A PARTY
On Sunday 15th August we invited our friends from Bermondsey. During the afternoon we played progressive cricket. After Benediction we all gathered in the library for dancing and some solo turns on the mike. We broke up about 10.30pm. Everybody must have had a good time because the question on leaving was 'When is the next one?' Among the visitors we have welcomed since June were Derek Aylett, Jimmy Florio, Frank Dennis, Tony Sayers, Jack Norman, John Howard, Johnnie Johnson, Pat Heffernan, Joe Gannon, Pat Brody, Kneale Oxton and John O'Brien. Christopher Stewart, more usually known as Jock, has since joined the Brothers of St. John of God. We assure him of our very sincere wishes and prayers for his perseverance. This is an order of Nursing Brothers; a very old one. They run hospitals for the chronically sick, Mental Hospitals and Homes for Boys. It is wonderful work. By the way, no amateurs these Brothers, who are qualified nurses etc.

Derek Aylett during his visit showed us some of the results of his Glass Blowing. Keep blowing, Derek. Mike Sheridan hopes to come on leave on the 12th Sept. and has his first stripe. Tony Sayers is transferring to the Military Police. The last time we saw him he must have been 6ft. 2". Frank Dennis has moved from Blanford and is now at Harwich attached to HQ Movement Cl. John Howard is being discharged from the RASC within a few weeks.

PLAYERS PLEASE BY JONNIE JOHNSON
If you had stayed at St. Mary's farm over the August Holiday you would have undoubtedly been asked to play or take part in a Cricket Match, which would have lingered in your memory for a long time. It surely must have been the most dramatic played at Underhills. You may have called it a Test Match Underhills style. Whether as a player or a spectator, you would have enjoyed every minute of it. The teams were composed of staff and Boys, sometimes called students, among many other things.

Although the match was only a suggestion by Father, the response was staggering. I might add that Father put his heart and soul into preparing for the pitch for what he knew was to be the event of the year. I only hope his gallant rolling of the concrete-like turf, was not too back breaking a job. Representing the staff was Father, Our Superintendent Mr. Dill, Mr. Loverman, the Tomato Basher, Mr. Tractor Driver and Mr. Reilly, several old boys and yours truly to bring the total up to eight. The students team was led by Joe Power. The day was Sunday and perfect weather for cricket. And with the staff batting first, the battle commenced. Almost at once two wickets had gone for a "Burton" and two batsmen for four runs. The boys thought they had the game in the bag. Little did they know the staff were no "mugs" and were not standing for that Lark! Three, then four wickets down. I was dismissed for three well-earned runs. Father showed fine style in the first innings only to be dismissed with a fine ball from Joe Power. He excelled himself however in the next innings. Seventh man in was J. Dill who provided some first class entertainment by missing the ball time and time again. It struck a comedy note with both sides doubled up with laughing. Eventually he did hit it and cheers echoed round the field. During the first innings he stayed in the longest and achieved nothing! Our remaining wickets soon fell with a total score of 24 runs. They exclaimed they had us veterans beaten. We made them eat their words. Batting went well for the boys in their first innings due to the superb batting of Jack Norman and Joe Power. Even Richard Knowler showed us to use both sides of the bat. Our bowling was slow but it got them in the end. Jimmy Florio's nut crackers made us keep our heads down. He must have thought he was on H.M.S. Glory playing basketball. Being wicket keeper for the staff my life was in some jeopardy and I found it was necessary to make a couple ejaculations as he sent fast "yorkers" down. And so 20 runs down we went into our second innings. By this time the pangs of hunger were upon us, yet those runs had to be got! John O'Brien did much better this time, assisted by slogger Jimmy Florio. Already our runs were mounting and their bowling was less menacing. Mr. Loverman and Mr. Lawrence showed the young "guns" what men of their age could do. Mr. Dill showed his hidden talent by knocking up a couple of fours. With twenty runs past our target our final batsmen went on to make sixty. A point about the last two. Father and Mr. Reilly between them put up a fine show of batsmanship, achieving the highest score. At least Father did! He was the Dennis Compton of the day, scoring over 20 runs. Well done, Father!

After tea and Benediction the boys had their second innings. Their wickets fell fast. Between Father and Mr. Lawrence these two took 75% of the wickets. The innings took about half an hour. The staff being victorious. Indeed it was a grand game and immensely enjoyed by everyone. It was a great pity that some of the lads at home and in Germany could not be here. I hope my simple report will bring your thoughts nearer to all who keep you in their thoughts at St. Mary's Farm. On behalf of all the boys who played I say thank you to Father, Mr. Dill and Mr. Loverman and all who helped to make it such an enjoyable afternoon. And so as your Sports Reporter I sign off and send best wishes to all our old boys wherever they are.

Be good.

J. W. Johnson

THANKS JOHNNIE FOR THE ABOVE

I know how long it must have taken you to write it. JOHN is our most loyal contributor. He has never failed to write a report when I have asked him. The last one was over six pages of notepaper. It probably took him the best part of an evening. The report is not done for me but for all the old boys to bring us closer together, although we are scattered round the world.

Here are two addresses I think you may not have:
J/SP. Heffernan P. / SS951121. J538 Mess. HMS Ocean. c/o GPO London.
23225365. Trpr. Hughes. MT Troop. HQ Sqdrn. 8RTR. BOAR 16

We are getting a collection of photographs of the family, but there are some more to come. What about it, you slow ones? Father is away at the moment at Dymchurch with St. Anne's and they are having wonderful weather. Many of you must have memories of Dymchurch. The boys from St. Joseph's are on the Isle of Wight. Father Davis is down with them for a week.

KOKO EMAILS, cont'd

Corrine and Bernie,

I can just imagine the Pope bragging to the Cardinals that he had a good sight of you both! Saw Tony Larkin yesterday and Michael Monaghan on Thursday. Alfred Cooke jr AKA Patrick Slevin has also been in touch after an absence of a few years.

Look after yourselves.

Josie and John

Hi John,

The Pope sends his blessings to you both via me and Corrine.

Bernie

Caroline,

I don't think I thanked you for my lovely birthday card and the cash – coin (Two Pounds), so 'Thank You.'

Josie is very impressed with your work which is indistinguishable from the "professional" authors. In fact she considers many books to be inferior with hardly any effort made to appeal to the customers when it comes to presentation. Josie has been away for a few days for a well needed respite. She returns tomorrow and I am rushing around rearranging the dust and hanging out the dirty washing.

I miss her but it has given me a chance to catch up with my emails. The job I have been working on "Down at the Farm" is taken from a tatty old

1950s Gestetner rolled off on to rotten copies! Which I had to retype to make them anyway respectable for our readers. If I didn't know what hard work you do with all that typing I certainly do now!

Take care of yourself.

John

Caroline,

Far as I am aware Irena's donation was from her own resources and has no connection with John O'D or anyone else. Yes, of course, I do remember Susan Tananbaum and her writings. I do recall stopping at a restaurant to join her for coffee.

So pleased that everything has gone so well for you. Had a good day with Terry yesterday on another of his flying visits. He is always welcome here.

KOKO as always, Caroline.

Josie and John

RE: POLICE ENQUIRY – ST. ANNE'S CONVENT, JULY 2015

Reply to Emma K Hill, Met. Police, UK.

Hi Emma,

Although most unexpected it was very nice to chat on the phone regarding the above matter. You should have by now received both the PDF files we talked about. I do hope you find time to read them (in your own time, of course) and would be delighted to know what you think of my little story and also "The Boys of St. Mary's", which I helped with in a little way, collating emails roughly over a two year period.

Many thanks.

Terry McKenna…

TASMANIA – DATED: 12 AUGUST, 2015

Michael Monaghan was over here from Tasmania. Everything is fine with him. Although he is over seventy years of age he is still working and tells me he loves it. He sees our emails occasionally via his son as he does not have a computer. Michael is one of the few who has no regrets about being shipped to Australia. He has made a success of his life and has a lovely wife and family. He has researched and met up with family over here and comes over at frequent intervals. I wouldn't be surprised if he were to place an order for a couple of "St. Mary's Boys" books.

The other Michael Monaghan is popping over to see us on Thursday and to collect two of "The Boys of St. Mary's" books which I mentioned to Caroline, previously.

We went to a wedding on Saturday. The family I stayed with in the fifties; their son was getting married, and another member of the family has bought one of our books.

If John Michael Murray or any of our number were to write a sequel to their stories, I feel they will have a "hit" on their hands. Each writer has their own inimitable style but all have what it takes to hold the reader's interest.

KOKO.

(Delvin) John Flynn

Caroline,

Just a thought! Sex is like a Rottweiler. They are fine if kept under control but havoc can prevail if control fails. The same with an Army. Discipline is "key", but again when they are allowed to run amok it's all very different. For example: In the seventies, the Paratroopers, who are a great body of men, rioted, and what was to be forever known as "Bloody Sunday" when they killed thirteen unarmed protesters.

Think on, and KOKO.

John.

Hi John and Caroline,

Just thought you might like to be updated with regard to our "friends" at Diagrama Foundation. As an exercise I thought I'd take a look at their "Home Page". My first result was: Diagrama's Children's Services. Anchorage House, 45-47 High Street, Chatham, Kent. ME4 4QG. Tel. 01582 583354.

Diagrama is now listed as the Vital Record Search though there is no additional Tel. Number for this service at all. Also listed at the same address is: Diagrama Hassockfield Ltd: Diagrama Rainsbrook Ltd. Telephone Area Code listed for this site is 01582 and is actually for Dunstable in Bedford despite a Medway Town address under Diagrama Foundation. 5th Floor, Anchorage House, High Street, Chatham, Medway, ME4 4LE. Tel. 01634 545000. (01634 is a Medway Town Area Code). On site there are lots of photos. Even the elusive Nathan Ward! Though none of the former staff we knew for many years including Ian Forbes, who John and I met at our meeting at Chez Flynn. This site also states that Diagrama have moved all their operations to the address above.

John, not sure if you wish to send these updated details to the rest of our group, though you will note I have sent this also to Caroline.

Caroline, I met with your friend Marion last week and she is doing remarkably well; albeit, using two walking sticks. She is scheduled to move into her new home by the end of the month and as soon as I know her address details I will pass them on to you, including her new telephone number and email address. Really hope your vertigo has gone! And things are back to normal. (This could never be said of me, could it!). Send my regards to your family. My brother Shaun is making a rare visit to the West country and my home, for a brief stop on his way to Exeter for some work, so that will be nice.

He's hoping to arrive about 15.30 on Sunday.

Cheers for now.

KOKO.

Terry McK...

Hi Terry,

Many thanks for your email. It is, as you and the rest of the group know, very important to keep on top of the activities of Diagrama, including Nathan Ward. It was our understanding from Ian Forbes (Cabrini) that our records were to be moved to Anchorage House in Chatham in 2016. What prompted this sudden rush? Now we need to know the person to contact if any member with their families wish to inspect their files. I take it John was not consulted as well as yourself by Diagrama of this move?

Coram, an unheard of organization, according to Elaine Brewster, is being asked by Diagrama for their advice how they store their records. I wonder if this has been carried out or is deemed unimportant enough for them to dwindle with results and thus has been dropped since our last communication with them ceased. Perhaps, John, it might be worth trying to contact David McGuire to find out the contact person for accessibility to OUR records? Where are they now actually stored, if at all.

Glad to hear Marion is making progress with her walking sticks. I did write a while ago but as yet, no response.

Antony Hayman emailed and he thoroughly enjoyed the book, now on loan to his neighbour.

Take care.

KOKO.

Caroline

Hi Caroline,

I will chat to John later to see if he wants to find out who our contact will be. If not, I will check. Not too bothered about Ian Forbes whereabouts because I really didn't trust him anyway, as you know.

Will let you know what I find.

Marion did say she had received your letter and I think as soon as she has moved in she will write to you. I now have "The Boys of St. Mary's" on Ebook. Younger brother Shaun did pay me the promised visit on his way to Exeter yesterday (Sunday), his first visit here in a decade. He was very interested in the size of the flat and the two bedrooms. So that was nice!

KOKO

Terry McK…

Terry,

It sounds as though Ian Forbes may have disappeared from the scene at Diagrama; perhaps due to the distance to travel from Purley to Chatham. If he was the link to accessibility of OUR records, who then do we contact if there is no phone number? It appears no-one from Cabrini has joined Diagrama at this new address.

John emailed pictures of some of the group at a reunion yesterday at Gravesend. Everyone looked good and well dressed. Wish I had been able to attend.

KOKO.

Take care.

Caroline

Hi John & Josie,

Hope your stay in Wales was a pleasant one. Just to let you know I recently purchased the book "The Boys of St. Mary's" and hope to receive it in time for Christmas. I am not expecting my name to be mentioned but no doubt there will be much else of interest to read from former pupils.

Merry Xmas and a Happy New Year to you both.

Love.

Patrick and Dawn

Response:

I hope you enjoy the book. Caroline has accomplished a difficult task of marrying up stories and emails of our time at St. Mary's, Gravesend.

We wish you and Dawn a Happy Christmas.

KOKO.

Josie and John

John,

Hmmm… a thought came to me. Does anyone remember a boy called Michael Spragg? At some time in the 1950s he left St. Mary's and went to Canada. I think he was adopted by a family there. I have no idea if he was an incomer from another residential Home or if he began schooling at St. John's.

Apologies, John, I haven't yet made that call to you. It may be an age thing? I must write myself a note.

KOKO.

Regards to you and Josie.

Michael Monaghan

Michael,

The name sounds familiar but I can't remember about him leaving for Canada. Does anyone remember Douglas Carol? His mother turned up and took him to the USA. I remember Sister Anthony when we were about nine years of age reading a letter to all the class (all letters were opened and censored) from Douglas's mother. She asked in the letter what food he liked. Did he want one or two pillows. This left us all with our jaws dropping. What was this thing called "choice"? We got what we were given and as they used to say "like it or lump it."

(Delvin) John Flynn

Hi All!

Hope you will forgive me for sending a joint email to you all but I just wanted to wish you (and anyone who knows me in the KOKO group) a very Happy Christmas and all the best – especially good health – in the New Year.

KOKO.

Take care and keep up the good work.

Irena Lyczkowski

Irena,

Lovely to receive your Christmas greetings and much acceptable to our group who, through John, also sent the same message to wish everyone a Happy Christmas, Good Health and Happiness in the New Year. To keep in touch with us means a great deal to those who have met you and who know you fully understand how important it is for us to "protect our own family" and support each other in every way. The camaraderie with the group is second to none. We are lucky with John still at the helm. Terry continues to upgrade his files, should we decided to do a sequel to "Boys". Although I have not yet put the idea to John I would like to hear stories of when the boys left St. Mary's to begin a new life of their own. They must have some unique experiences to share.

I hope you are keeping well and enjoying your new environment in London.

My best to you and your family at Christmas and the New Year, 2016.

God Bless.

Caroline, Canada

Hi Delvin,

Wishing your group a Happy Christmas and a good New Year.

I read all the emails, with interest.

KOKO.

Regards.

Tony Ledger

Tony,

Thanks, and a very Happy Christmas to you!

KOKO.

See you soon.

John

John,

Your comment re: choice epitomizes our situation Chez St. Mary's. Do you remember Mrs Crundle? (have probably misspelled it?) With the benefit of hindsight she resembled the Grandma character in the Giles cartoons. She was responsible for general sweeping stairs and corridors. A somewhat foreboding person.

Have a super Christmas. My thoughts go to those unfortunates in Cumbria.

Glen

Glen,

It was Miss Cromwell and she travelled to the school each day from her home in Singwell Road, Gravesend. You have got it right about her being in charge of the cleaning.

Have a Happy Christmas, Glen.

(Delvin) John Flynn

Greetings From John

Happy Christmas To St. Mary's Boys Group.

Josie and John

Dear John and Josie,

Here's a snapshot of Roger Simmons and Tony Larkin.

Speak later.

Ann

Ann,

That's our Tony! Tony was a tad older than me and when we left St. Mary's he used to return and treat me to the cinema. He doesn't remember his kindness or was he being just modest.

Historians generally retain information.

KOKO

Love,

J.

GREETINGS FROM AUSTRALIA

We wish you and Josie and your family a Happy Christmas.

Greetings to all the St. Mary's Boys Group.

Best Wishes for the New Year.

Pat and Mavis Heffernan

Hello John and Josie,

Lovely greetings from Pat and Mavis.

Canada too sends all the Very Best for the New Year and wishes them and all our group of writers, health and happiness in the coming year.

The shore fires in Australia I trust, are now under control. The news here did not quote which part of Australia was experiencing these dreadful fires.

Hope everyone is well.

Caroline

Hello Caroline,

The recent bush fires on Christmas Day were along the coast in Victoria, about 30 miles from us. The fires are in dense bush land and will probably burn for weeks as they are hard to access. Luckily no lives were lost but 116 homes were destroyed.

Best wishes to everyone.

Pat and Mavis

Pat and Mavis,

I take it whilst you are concerned for those who lost their homes in the fire, you and yours are safe?

I haven't heard from Tony Blanchfield for some time but since he is hundreds of miles away from you and Victoria State, living in Queensland, he is not only safe but I hope had a very happy Christmas.

Tony, as you know, enjoys the simple life, fixing his boats and toughing it with his like-minded friends. Michael Vaughan visited this country a couple of years ago, calling on Tony Larkin but he has not made contact since. I wonder if he gets our emails?

Rob and Sue Tyrrell contact us on Skype from Western Australia. Rob went over there as a mere 10-year-old so can't have too many memories of St. Mary's. Then there are the Monaghans living in Tasmania, so you might say we are reasonably well represented in Australia Land!

KOKO

John F

John,

Firstly, this message is priceless! I believe the writer's description of the lady in black who worked at St. Mary's was the same person who gave a young John Michael Murray the job of cleaning the stairs, and was always regarded as a grumpy old soul.

Actually, going back a few eras, I remember my husband's grandmother always wore a long black dress over which was a pristine starched white apron. This lady held me in awe throughout the time I knew her and despite being a miner's wife, was the ultimate in stretching a pound or two on a pittance of a wage. Not many of her breed today know the meaning of maintaining a good home or how to feed a family. Somehow, worldwide, we have all gone "to pot".

As a child I remember being up at the crack of dawn, to attend mass.

Often the St. Anne's girls nodded off during the service, only to be sharply poked in the back and told 'pay attention', by a Nun. If we coyly stretched our necks to look at the St. Joseph's boys sitting on the other side of the aisle in the church, also bleary eyed, we noticed the hand of one of the Brothers come smack-down on their heads. Such were the past joys of attending mid-night mass.

I know Terry is filing all emails from the group.

Take care as always.

KOKO

L & H's to you and Josie.

Caroline

John,

Your message was compelling with regard to Tony Larkin. In the analysis, it is each to his own; although many of us often fail in religious events we do still care deeply about what our childhood upbringing taught us. To survive the many hurdles we needed to cross in our adult years had we not been given this advantage I cannot begin to imagine where or to whom we would turn, in time of need, without our religious training. It is a subject of thought for all time. Personally, without the guiding hand, I firmly believe I could not have achieved all I aimed for, to ensure a better life.

With L & H's.

Caroline

Hi John & Josie,

Interesting to read your email re: Photo and Tony Larkin. Do you know the history behind it? The only recollection I have of a photo and Tony Larkin is the one of Pious XI. Are we on the same track?

Love to you both and a Happy New Year.

Pat Slevin

Pat and Clare,

There was a picture I think that was discovered on a market stall of a Pope (Pious the XII, I think) and inscribed on the picture was a blessing to the children and cares of St. Mary's. Tony knows all the details but as I have mentioned previously he isn't on the Internet so communication is slow. They don't call the post "snail mail" for nothing! Actually, the post isn't too bad, but it can't compete with email.

Happy New Year to you and yours.

KOKO.

Josie and John

John,

This one is totally priceless! Have not had breakfast yet. I think I should stop writing to restore laughter and energy.

I do hope Terry is keeping a record of this one for the book?

KOKO

L & H's.

Caroline

December 31, 2015

MEMORIES OF ST. MARY'S, GRAVESEND

A very proud Pat Heffernan (centre) January 2016.

BY PATRICK HEFFERNAN

When I think back to the Nuns, the Sisters of Charity at Gravesend, I always remember the saying we used to have: The Sisters of Charity had no mercy and the Sisters of Mercy had no charity. It wasn't true of all the Sisters. However, I do very much recall that Sister Gerard had a straight right and left Muhammed Ali would have been proud of. I know this as they were aimed at me once or twice. Sister Gerard was the only Nun I could never get along with. It may be just a coincidence that her dislike of me started a few years before she was appointed as Sister Superior of St. Mary's, Gravesend. It was at the time when a previous Sister Superior Catherine (or Vincent, I am not too sure of the name) was moved to the head office of the Sisters of Charity in London. Sister

Catherine (or Vincent), along with (I believe) Father Baker came into the junior refectory when we were having a meal. They were accompanied by our beloved Sister Patricia and Sister Gerard. We had never seen Sister Gerard before that day. It was put to us by Father Baker we were to have a new Reverend Mother and were asked who we wanted in that position, Sister Patricia or Sister Gerard. All of the boys in unison screamed out Sister Patricia. I along with some of the other boys started to bang on the table with our mugs and spoons chanting, we want Sister Patricia. It built up quite a crescendo. I recall most vividly seeing Sister Gerard glaring at me as she left the room. She never took her eyes off me. Never in my wildest dreams did I realize that in two years Sister Gerard would end up as the Reverend Mother. Just my luck!

One really horrible experience I can still remember quite clearly, is when I was about eight or nine. I was sent for from the playing yard at St. Mary's and told to go up to the dormitory and change into my Sunday best clothes. I was escorted by one of the Nuns to the reception room because, as I was told, my mother had come to visit me. I always had a good memory of what my mother looked like from a couple of visits to me at Liphook and in Baldock. As I entered the reception room the Reverend Mother was standing with a woman who I immediately said was not my mother. It was realized there was another Patrick Heffernan at the school and it turned out to be his mother. I was sent back to change and to return to the yard with the other boys. It was very disappointing and that moment has remained with me even today. This type of event was not unusual at St. Mary's, with a number of parents turning up occasionally out of the blue to see their sons.

AFTER ST. MARY'S

My exist from St. Mary's turned out to be a very big disappointment for Reverend Mother Sister Gerard. Long before my departure another boy William Gillespie, for reason unknown to me, was expelled for crimes he was supposed to have committed and was sent to St. Joseph's in Orpington, run by the Irish Brothers. We were reminded time after time by Sister Gerard and one or two of the other Nuns that Gillespie cried and begged not to be taken from St. Mary's to St. Joseph's, Orpington. (There was a strong possibility there were no witnesses to the "crime" alleged by Father Baker and Sister Gerard.) It was used as an attempt to strike fear into us boys, or me in particular. There was no love lost between Sister Gerard and myself, as I explained earlier.

I have obtained copies of letters written between Sister Gerard, Canon Arbuthnott and Brother Euseblus as well as of all people, Mr. S.A. Bray. At the time Mr. Bray was headmaster of St. John's, Denton (until he did a midnight bunk to Australia with his family). It was alleged he helped himself to a large amount of school funds. These letters showed that plans were well in advance for me to go to Orpington.

On the day of my departure I was instructed to go up to the dormitory and to collect any personal things I possessed. Nothing, but my Sunday clothes and boots! Then I was to join Sister Madeline and David Jordan in the back of Father Baker's jeep (CAN 161). The main reason for this was so they could witness me doing a Gillespie – begging, crying and pleading not to be removed from St. Mary's and taken to Orpington. I was never told I was being transferred to Orpington. I just guessed! I had even worked out the presence of Sister Madeline and David Jordan had been included. History was repeating itself regarding Gillespie. I fully remember when it came to the time to leave for me and the escort party. If looks could kill Sister Gerard would have had me hung drawn and quartered there and then. Not once did I give them the satisfaction of crying, begging or any other emotions. In fact on arrival at Orpington, I recognized a couple of the boys from a previous trip to Dymchurch and gave them a cheery hello.

Like Queen Victoria, Sister Gerard was not amused. Dear old Father Baker put his arm round my shoulder, shook my hand and told me to look after myself. The two years I spent at Orpington were a good experience. I, like all the other lads, got into trouble. Sometimes I was caught, but the Brothers were always fair and firm. In 1954 I left to go to Bletchingly to try farming at Underhills Farm in Surrey. I loved the farm and Bletchingly but right from the start I had reservations concerning spending my life being a farmer. I had for many years a desire to go to sea. I wasn't overly keen on farm work in the middle of winter with snow and frost about. Getting up at 4am. to round up the cows and taking them for milking and cleaning up after they had been turned back into the fields or yards. After breakfast there were all the other chores which needed to be done. Depending on the season, it could be ploughing the fields, sowing seeds, digging up potatoes and bagging them, or loading bales of hay or straw and stacking them. Also there was the market garden to learn and attend to, mostly in the large greenhouse controlled by Mr. Jim Loverman. A very good friend of Canon Arbuthnott, Mr. Jerry Dill was the house manager and superintendent. He and his wife looked after the house and controlled us lads. There was also a large pig sty which took a lot of looking after.

After several months of training in all facets of basic farming, Jerry Dill and Canon Arbuthnott arranged for the boys to be sent out to various farms in the country for full time employment. I was sent out to a farm in Mayfield, Sussex. It was owned by a former Colonial civil servant who had spent a considerable number of years in India. His name was Alistair Cecil Roy Cuncliffe-Mitchard. The big problem with this man was, I think, he considered he was still living in India and the farm staff were his sepoys, to follow his orders. As a 15-year-old I found it very difficult to accept working 14 hours a day, six and a half days a week, for a few shillings. In the end I visited Canon Arbuthnott at Underhills Farm, informing him I had no interest or desire to be a farmer and wished to join the Navy. Canon Arbuthnott arranged for me to go and live at the hostel in Blackheath, from where I signed on for the Navy in the recruiting office, just up the road from the hostel, in December 1954.

On the 17 February 1955 I became a sailor in Her Majesty's Royal Navy. Hello, Sailor!

MORE MEMORIES OF ST. MARY'S, GRAVESEND

One of the enduring memories I have is the number of times I climbed the wire fence around the play yard alongside Glen View. Some of us would sneak into the section nearby, which was an orchard and where Father Baker kept his bees. We called it "scrumping" and used to place any apples and pears down the front of our shirts. One time after having a good "scrump" I was caught by a fairly new, very tall Nun, whose name was Sister Catherine (we previously had another Sister Catherine) who was on guard duty. She took me by the ear and marched me down to the school to Sister Gerard's office and reported me. I was then made to kneel down on the concrete floor outside the office. I ended up there for about three hours. Every now and then Sister Gerard would check on me. If she caught me sitting on the floor and not kneeling I got a whack on the ears.

I even still smile when the memory comes to me. All because Sister Catherine had not observed on the way down from the school yard, I had managed to lob some of the apples and pears into the shrubbery near the path; she was always unaware that I had any fruit at all. I had broken the rules by climbing out of the yard and had to be punished. When I was handed over to Sister Gerard I still had a number of apples and pears down the front of my shirt, which neither of the Nuns noticed.

I spent most of the three hours enjoying eating my ill-gotten gains.

OTHER MEMORIES

Another big coincidence in my life was in 1969. I met and got engaged to a young lady who was travelling back to Australia after visiting relatives in England. When she was a young girl, her family had moved to Australia. I wonder if any of the lads can recall a Nun with the name of Sister Genevieve, some time after 1953. I believe she did two spells of duty at St. Mary's. I first met Sister Genevieve in late 1969. I drove all the way from Gravesend (where I had a flat) to Liverpool, to meet her in the Convent the Nuns owned. Also, there was Sister Madeline. The big coincidence was that Sister Genevieve was the aunt of the girl to whom I became engaged. Her father was one of Sister Genevieve's brothers. The two other brothers also lived in Melbourne. Both were lawyers. One, Percy, was a solicitor and the other, Peter, was a Queen's Counselor.

Seven years later, we divorced, and had major legal battles in the Family Court over custody and access to our daughter.

I remarried to a good one!

THE SKYLARK ON WINDMILL HILL

BY JOHN MICHAEL MURRAY

Old legs, tired legs, legs that had known better times took me slowly along the red dusty path to the foot of a small hill where the cemetery lay. The Australian sun was doing its best to dissuade me from making the climb, but I had come this far and I could not and I would not be beaten. I had made a promise to Chris over sixty years ago on a cold day in January 1953 we would meet again one day, and today was that day. Clutching a bottle of water in one hand, gripping my walking stick with the other, I inched slowly up the hill. The heat, the climb, and the old age conspired to exhaust the remains of what energy I had left. The cemetery was small, just a few crosses and headstones, most uncared for, no flowers, only weeds and red dust. Here Chris was buried.

It had been a long journey, one that I had made many times in my mind and now it was over. I left a cold England in February, a long uncomfortable flight. Chris had come by ship, with hundreds more orphans to be settled in the schools, the orphanages and the homesteads of this vast country. I wanted to go, but for reasons unknown to me at the time I was left behind. Finding Chris's grave was not easy, but find it I did. A simple wooden cross with a faded epitaph was all that was left of his life. "Chris Chapel, August 1943 – 19 July 1964". I tidied the grave the best my arthritic hands would allow, then rested on a convenient old log.

'Hello, Chris, I kept my promise. I got here as soon as I could, please forgive me for taking so long. I had difficulty finding you. I asked the Nuns in the orphanage at Gravesend but they would not tell me. As I grew older I contacted the Church, the Salvation Army and Social Services. I've lost count of the number of people to whom I wrote; they were unwilling to give me any information regarding what happened to you. I know now it was a shame that kept them silent. I eventually found you, thanks to the Internet, and here I am. Over the years I often thought of you, wondering what you were doing, whether you liked Australia. I read that a lot of you were badly treated. I hoped you were not one of them, you had enough bad treatment in Gravesend. When I learned of your death I was so sad. I lit a candle and said a prayer for you in the local church just in case nobody else had.'

I took a sip from what remained of the water; the heat and the dust were drying my throat.

'Can you remember the time we sneaked out of the playground and went to Windmill Hill to find bird nests? It was a lovely sunny day, we ran up the hill through the long grass making as much noise as eight-year-old boys were capable of. The tall grass stinging our bare legs. We wore grey shorts, long trousers were forbidden, and we were a long way off that. We rolled in the grass, having pretend fights, then we would chase each other. I could never catch you, you were a better runner than me. When we were tired, we sat and ate our jam sandwiches we pinched from the kitchen and drank lemonade made with sherbert powder in an old Tizer bottle.

'We counted the ships on the Thames where there used to be dozens, lots of Navy boats, but there's none now. The hospital ship is still there. We were told when it was flying a yellow flag somebody had "yellow jack" whatever that was. We searched in the bushes for bird's nests. I know now it was wrong but it was good fun at the time and we did learn a lot about birds. Can you remember watching the soldier with his girlfriend lying under a blanket?

'You said they were 'doing it,' though we did not know what 'doing it' was.

'He heard us giggling and chased us. When he caught up with us he offered a sixpence each if we would go away and not bother him. We felt rich! We could see the Orphanage from the top of the hill. It's not there now; it was knocked down and they have built houses. When we heard the Angelus bell ringing we knew we had to go back. We walked through the tall grass, slowly, then we saw it, the Skylark, our first Skylark. It rose from the ground and started singing, getting higher and higher, all the time singing.

The higher it went, the louder it seemed to sing, even when it was just a little black dot high in the sky it was still singing. We lay on our backs, shielded our eyes from the sun and watched it until we could not see or hear it anymore.

'You said, 'It was like a soul going up to heaven.'

'Years later, when I took my grandchildren into the countryside, every time we heard a Skylark I would tell them it was Chris going to heaven.

'We were late back and got caught by Sister Louise who gave us the cane for sneaking out. We didn't care; we had seen the Skylark and we each had sixpence. Soon you went away. In January 1953, they took you to Australia. We both cried and promised to see each other again. The Nuns put you on a coach with the other boys and the last I saw of you was through the coach window. That night I looked at your empty bed and cried myself to sleep. The next morning we were taken to the upstairs dormitory and told to look out of the window and wave. There was a ship, moving slowly down the Thames and out to sea. We watched until it got smaller and smaller and just like the Skylark, it was gone.'

I sat, head bowed, along with my thoughts, saying long forgotten prayers from my Catholic past.

The peace was ended, replaced by the sound of a strong Aussie voice. 'You OK, mate?'

I looked up before answering. 'Yes, thanks, I'm fine.'

'What yer doing up here? I heard yer talking and by the sound of yer, you're a long way from home.'

I looked at him, unsure whether to answer, but I did.

'I'm fulfilling a promise to a friend. That's his grave.'

'You sure, mate? That's my granddad.'

He took off his hat and wiped his brow, revealing a head of fine blond hair, his eyes were a striking blue, the image of Chris.

'You look like him,' I said.

'Did you know my granddad?'

'Yes, many years ago, in a different time and a different place.'

'Look, mate, it's getting late. I've got my truck at the bottom of the hill, let me give you a ride back to town.'

'Thank you, that would be most kind,' I replied.

I took one last look at the grave and after a whispered 'Goodbye, Chris, see you soon,' we left the cemetery.

'Fancy a beer, mate, you look done in? I know somebody who would like to meet you.'

It had been a long day and I was tired but I felt I could not refuse the offer. I'll never pass this way again.

'Good on yer, mate, it's not far.'

A twenty-minute drive took us to a homestead. Compared to others I had seen on the way, this one looked substantial, stone built and surrounded by a well-tended garden.

'Come in, mate, have yourself a seat.'

I was thankful for the coolness of the room and the comfort of the leather armchair he offered me.

'Let me get you a beer.'

I heard him shout, 'Dad come here, I've got someone I'd like you to meet.'

He returned with three beers and a man, judging from his blond hair and blue eyes, who was his father.

'Dad, I met this gentleman up at Granddad's grave, says he knew him.'

He moved towards me, hand out ready to shake mine.

'Hello, mate, you knew my dad?'

'Yes,' I said, feeling the firmness of his handshake. I could tell he was suspicious; perhaps not trusting me.

'I'm George, this is my son Chris, named after his granddad.'

'What's your name, mate?'

'Just call me Mike,' I said.

The two of them looked at each other, surprise clearly showing on their faces.

'Drink your beer, Mike, and let's talk.'

I began to tell them all I knew of my friend Chris, how we had spent six years together in an orphanage in Gravesend. The atmosphere became more relaxed as I spoke. I declined another beer and carried on talking, answering their many questions.

'Do you know when Chris was born 'cause we don't?' George asked.

'The third of August 1943, two days before me; he used to tease me because he was the older. We went to the orphanage at the same time when we were about three-years-old. I came from a Home in Brighton; nobody knew where Chris came from. The Nuns told Chris he was found in a chapel with a note attached to him saying his name was Chris so they called him "Chapel".'

Their interest never waned, finding more questions to ask, wanting to know everything. I had to remind them I was an old man now and some memories fade.

'Tell me about Chris here in Australia,' I asked.

George began by saying he knows nothing of his father other than he worked at this cattle station. 'He was taken on for the annual round up as they were short of hands. He was young, fit and a good worker. He had a young wife who was pregnant at the time. They kept themselves to themselves, living in one of the shacks. The other hands liked him and thought he was a ten pounds Pom looking to make a new life over here. They know nothing of what you have told us. Anne – his wife and my mother – died in childbirth. Chris was killed some days later when the truck he was driving hit a tree. I was four weeks old at the time.' He paused before continuing. 'The station owner and his wife adopted me. They couldn't have children of their own so I grew up here. When they died I inherited the station. They told me what little they knew of Chris, but until now he had always been a mystery. I thank you for what you have told us.'

Chris spoke, looking directly at me. 'When I found you at the cemetery you were talking to your friend. What were you saying?'

'Steady on, Chris,' said his father. 'What sort of question is that to ask?'

'That's all right,' I said. 'I was reminiscing of our time together, the fun we had and the sadness of our parting.'

They listened in silence as I told them about our time on Windmill Hill. George motioned with his head to his son, who left the room. On his return, he was holding a folded piece of paper. It was well-thumbed and carried the signs of age. He handed it to me.

I looked at them both. 'What's this?' I asked.

'You might like to have it,' said George.

Slowly I unfolded the paper, my hands were shaking, my eyes watered, as I looked at the simple child-like drawing. There we were together. Chris had drawn a picture in pencil, a hill marked "Windmill Hill", two matchsticks figures, one marked "Mick", the other marked "Me". Above them was a bird with the word "Skylark".

"Drawn by Chris Chapel" was written across the bottom.

He had not forgotten. I could rest now!

LIFE AFTER ST. MARY'S

BY ANTONY HAYMAN

RETURNING FROM THE HOSPITAL

My mother and sister Freda whom I had not seen for six years, met me at Ashford Station. At that time I was on crutches which I soon abandoned. My first job was at a cycle warehouse but due to shortages this soon closed. Next job was in a factory making ploughshares. Being brought up by the good Sisters of St. Mary's, I was totally unfamiliar to the industrial language used. When I told my mother she took me away from there and instead sent me to work in an hotel on the seafront of Folkestone. Shortly after I left the agricultural factory it was bombed and most of the men I had worked with were killed.

Fate works in mysterious ways, doesn't it?

Folkestone was being heavily shelled by the big guns across the Channel so we were constantly having to retreat to the cellars. I was front-of-house porter and part of my job was to wait on customers, taking drinks orders and hoping for tips. This, despite my Italian heritage, proved much too servile for me and I looked for a change. One happening which hastened my departure was concerning an Army Officer. Remember my Catholic upbringing had taught me nothing about sex so when the Captain said there was something wrong with the toilet, unthinkingly, I followed him in. Well, he then patted my bottom!

What instinct took over I have no idea but I shot out of there like a bullet out of a gun. I went down to the basement and refused to come back up, much to the amusement of the staff and customers.

I wrote to my brother Tom and he answered to come and live with him in Surrey. There he managed to get me in a factory making part of a mortar bomb. This was night work so I bed swapped with my brother who was a Head Dairyman.

This I did for about six months until I fell out with the Foreman. This rascal was having an affair in work time with a married woman whose husband was abroad in the Army. There was a caravan in the grounds where these two would go off to for their assignations. Part of my work was to get a long steel tube from the far end of the factory to cut up to form part of the mortar bomb. Putting this tube on my shoulder like Laurel and Hardy, I swung round and put one end right through the Time Clock glass.

The married woman was passing at the time and I said to her 'now I'm in trouble.' Whether she misheard what I said I don't know but she reported me to the Foreman who then threatened to beat me up. Being a Hayman I took up a heavy spanner to defend myself and he hurriedly backed off. The upshot of that was a meeting in the office and I resigned. More of this later.

LONDON

Now where was I? Oh, yes, I was in London, wasn't I?

I have to admit I was happy. I was treated like one of the large Italian family and Uncle Johnny, my employer, even gave me Birthday and Christmas gifts. Towards the end of my time there, when the War in Europe ended and Opera had resumed at Covent Garden, I was treated to a box all to myself to see and experience my first opera, Tosca.

I was in my seventh heaven.

Unfortunately, a good deed from Johnny resulted in my London episode being over. He knew about my osteomyelitis and arranged for me to see an Italian Doctor in Soho. This came about because I had had my call up papers. I went to my Physical and was given grade four because of my leg. The examining doctor asked if my own doctor had heard of Penicillin. I relayed this to Uncle Johnny and he arranged the aforementioned visit to the doctor. Result: I was sent to the Middlesex Hospital in Mortimer street where I was operated on by the brilliant Mr. White-Hudson. After two weeks and millions of Penicillin units I was cured of a disease I had had since 1940, which also had broken out on my left clavicle. However, the Consultant said working in an underground kitchen was unwise, so that finished my dead-end job.

I went to stay with my half brother in Newcross. John, who was a full Italian, had a vile temper so after a couple of months I went to stay, yet again, with my brother Tom in Surrey. I had a couple of jobs there before I was sent by the Agricultural board to work in a Garden Nursery in Gravesend. So I was back where I started.

I soon went to St. Mary's and found it radically changed.

I will continue with this story soon.

ANOTHER MOVE

I had left the bomb factory so I worked for a month on a farm doing all sorts of jobs. Unfortunately my old enemy osteomyelitis reared its ugly head and a large piece of dead bone (called sequestrum) decided to try and exit out of the side of my right leg. This resulted in a stay in the

Redhill hospital and an operation to remove said bone. So it was home to my dear mother who promptly dispatched me to London to work in an Italian friend's restaurant in Southampton Row. London was still being bombed at this time.

Perhaps Mother was trying to get rid of me.

Wartime was a very poor time for the catering trade because of food rationing so there was the occasional joint of beef or lamb and some sort of meat which looked suspiciously like horse meat and was heavily disguised as goulash. So I learned very little cooking.

YOUTHFUL PASSION

On a holiday from work I spent two weeks at home in Maidstone. My mother had separated from her second husband and become housekeeper(?) to an old farmer. The less said about that, the better.

I was nineteen and she was fifteen. For me it was love at first sight. I had gone to see some old friends and when I knocked on the door it was opened by this slip of a girl who looked at me with these amazingly clear grey eyes. I was lost!

We became friends and went to the cinema a couple of times and "snogged" a little, which I found somewhat disconcerting. However, things were about to change.

'Let me introduce you to my cousin Hazel.' This innocent remark was to have a profound effect on my life for the next six years. Off we went to an address in Maidstone, myself being somewhat reluctant. Well, I met this cousin and fell immediately in love. It felt like being hit on the head with a large piece of timber. I believe the French call it the *coup de foudre*. I remember it so well. Slim as a reed, with lovely honey blonde hair down to her waist, Hazel had the most beautiful clear grey eyes. Doesn't sound much does it, but I was smitten.

I was working in London at the time and Hazel lived in South Woodford. We went out for about nine months before I was unceremoniously dumped for the first time. I discovered by accident she had another boyfriend who was in the Army. I recall it vividly; the misty London streets and the lamplight glistening on the wet pavement. Many a night I missed the last bus and had to walk home, a distance of some five miles. Sometimes in the snow. At one time when crossing back over the river to Gravesend, I contemplated suicide but the water looked too cold. The madness of first love.

I will continue this later because it was not by far the end of the story.

LIFE IN LONDON

Firstly I was billeted with the family at a house in Mount Pleasant, not far from the big Post Office. The air raid sirens were always a noisy presence and one evening they sounded about nine o'clock. I tried to persuade the family to go into a surface shelter which was right outside the house but they said no, so we walked to a large office block opposite the main Post Office.

Loud explosions followed which shook the building. When the all clear sounded we went back to what little was left of the house and the shelter. So I was off to stay with another branch of the family in King's Cross road. There I met Luigi, a boy of my own age, and we became firm friends.

After this settled down Uncle Johnny Servini purchased a house in Calthorpe Street not far from Mount Pleasant and I lived in there with my new landlady who was Auntie Delina, Johnny's sister. I was very comfortable living in the house and I got on well with Delina who was a mature lady about fifty-years. While I was there Delina's brother and his family came down from Liverpool for two weeks holiday. His two children were Rene and Peter and we soon became good friends. Following their return to Liverpool, Rene and I corresponded for two years. Rene stayed at Delina's and we went the cinema a couple of times and we were getting on well. Alas, once again disaster struck. I remember the scene well. Rene and I were sitting on a settee in the basement lounge reading the newspaper. It was all about the first Atom Bomb on Hiroshima. It felt like the end of the world had come and then for some reason we came together for a kiss. Just at that moment Delina walked in and all hell broke loose. You would think we were on the floor, naked. Rene was immediately dispatched to stay with another sister in

Earl's Court. I only saw her once before the family returned to Liverpool. I never saw her again. I have never forgotten that kiss.

London in wartime was still a magical place to me. I visited Westminster Abbey, St. Paul's, Tower of London, Petticoat Lane and other historical places. The fact we could have been blown to pieces at any time did not worry us. We were willing and care-free.

I left London shortly after V.E. Day.

I was one of the huge crowd pressed up against the rails of Buckingham Palace and there when the Royal Family and Churchill appeared on the balcony. Never enough of it, bit like McArthur; I will return.

THE CHERRY TREES

Returning home to Maidstone following my year in Gravesend, my mother informed me that she had bought the cherries of two orchards in Charing. This was quite a common practice in Kent. There had to be someone on guard in the orchards in case of thieves and also to scare the birds away. I was elected to do this for a supposed share of the profits. I was given a tent, a two-bore shotgun, some cartridges and some provisions to keep me going. I had never slept in a tent before, much less handled a shotgun. But I was a St. Mary's boy so I got stuck in. I shot and killed rabbits, skinned them and cooked them over a fire. My mother appeared at weekends with more supplies.

The foolish part of this venture was that the two orchards were half a mile apart, so no sooner had I scared the birds from one site I had to run to the other orchard to do the same. A month of this I was worn out, but I did sleep well. To add to my woes it was the worst summer weather for years so at the end of the day when we picked the cherries, we made very little profit; in fact, taking in the cost of cartridges and food we were probably out of pocket.

Back home I had to find some employment. I had no qualifications and only a sketchy education. My mother prompted me to apply for a position with the local Bus Company, which I did. I heard nothing for a couple of weeks so I applied for a job at a Stationers and Printers in King Street, Maidstone. It was only to pack and dispatch finished print jobs.

I was always a hard and fast worker so I had time on my hands. On the same floor where I worked were an old fashioned ruling machine and the white paper guillotine. I soon learned all the different types of paper used and how to cut them into sizes for the printing machines. So much so that Mr. Baker the boss decided to purchase a small hand guillotine for me to work on.

I got on very well with the Manager, Mr. Coleman, who more or less took me under his wing, as did Mr. Posee, who was the main printers cutter. This went on for two or three months until one day the totally unexpected happened. Mr. Coleman had an almighty row with Mr. Posee which resulted in the latter walking off the job. Utter panic ensued because with no guillotine operator, the work would come to a standstill.

Step forward young Hayman, who said, 'I can do that job.'

My offer was accepted, and I was away. I made a success of the job and paid same rate as all the other printers. This included Compositers, Machine Operators and Binders. This occasioned a certain amount of jealousy because they had served seven years apprenticeships and I had not. However, I kept my head down and just got on with the work. So the years went on and I eventually became the Paper Buyer, as well.

I will have to leave this story there because I am getting ahead of myself.

About eighteen months into the job I had a further problem with my leg and was sent back to the Middlesex for a minor operation. I was lying in my hospital bed recovering from my operation, feeling sorry for myself, when down the ward walked Hazel's mother. After a brief exchange of pleasantries, she asked me if I would mind if Hazel came in.

Intrigued, I said, 'Okay.'

Hazel walked down the ward looking absolutely gorgeous and my heart somersaulted. To this day I have no idea how they knew I was in hospital. I came out of the hospital and stayed with them for a brief convalescence and my romance was rekindled. However I soon discovered Hazel was still engaged to her soldier boy but wanted to get back with me. Why didn't I think then if she was prepared to cheat on one man she would do the same with me. I felt I was in a somewhat invidious position. I did not want to give up on the chance of continuing my relationship, particularly as Hazel said she was trying to break off her engagement. My head was in such a whirl it never occurred to me I was being used for just that reason. I returned to Maidstone and work but I continued to go to London every weekend.

Some weeks Hazel came to Maidstone and stayed with her uncle and aunt. Our relationship became more physical especially when she broke off her engagement. I really thought this is it! What fools we are when we are in love. We eventually became engaged much too soon after her previous liaison, but I was afraid of losing her again. I will never forget the last weekend I spent in London. Everything seemed normal. We had been visiting another of her aunts in Wanstead. We stopped for a cigarette, and then she told me that she thought it had been a mistake to get engaged and we ought to have a break. I was so enraged I simply walked away from her.

She trailed behind me and I heard her say, 'Nobody will ever say the nice things you say to me.'

But I was too upset to listen. I collected my case from her house and caught a train back to Maidstone. Three months later my sister Freda came to see me at work, bringing with her a work colleague, Gwendoline White. Gwen looked very nice and had the cheek to ask for a date. I will be honest and say this was not the *coupe de foudre* of my previous liaison but over the next few months our love for each other grew. We have been happily married for nearly sixty-four-years, although the shadow of Hazel has never gone away. Not long after I had met Gwen I had a request from Hazel for a meet. What her intention was I don't know but during the meeting she asked if I had a girlfriend.

I replied, 'Yes,' and that was that!

Over the next fifty-years my anger towards her cooled, and certain meetings were unavoidable. Her uncle and aunt lived in Maidstone and when they died we met in passing at their respective funerals. When Hazel's sister Audrey died at just fifty-two, Hazel phoned to inform me. We kept in touch by phone after that and we visited them at their house in the Wickford area. I had no intention of visiting Hazel at home but feeling "pecked", I popped into a local pub for a beer and sandwich. Who should be laying the table, but Hazel.

You would have thought she would have said, 'Hello, Tony, what are you doing in the area?' but no, she looked across the room and said, 'Mum's had to go into a Home.'

She then walked across the room straight into my arms and we kissed. I hasten to add this was not the embrace of passion it once was but a kiss of deep understanding and sympathy.

We kept in touch until many years later when she was seventy-four and she told me she had terminal cancer. On the day before she died I phoned to see how she was. Her voice was low and hoarse and the last thing she asked, 'Do you still love me?'

What does one say to a dying woman who had once been dear to me? I replied a little vaguely with a favourite bit of Shakespeare's Sonnet: "Love is not love which alters when it(s) alteration finds, nor bends with The Remover to remove".

Not the best reply in the world, but to reply 'Yes, of course I do,' would have felt disloyal to my dear wife.

Hazel died the next day.

CHANGE NEEDED

Having worked at Vivish and Baker Printers for nearly sixteen years I felt I needed a change. I applied for the position of Shop Manager, when it became vacant, but was turned down on the basis I was so good at my job I would be hard to replace. Not good. I felt hard done by but I soldiered on. During this time the Print Union called a strike so I was out of work. I did all sorts of odd jobs to keep the wolf from the door but a perverse fate was waiting for me just around the corner. I was taken ill with peritonitis and came very close to the "Grim Reaper". No bed available at the Maidstone hospital so I was rushed to the Tunbridge Wells Hospital, a very bumpy ride. I survived but was off work for some weeks of recovery.

Then one day I was dealing with a paper merchant who advised me that an office position had become available with a neighbouring firm. I applied and got the job. Not the best move I have made because Mr. Smith, the owner, was a very mean man. No overtime pay in the office.

Sometimes because I had been "saddled" with the wages, I worked eleven hours a day.

A year after I moved there my son Paul was born. Great joy, but no pay rise! We were struggling a bit so when I got home from work about six, Gwen would go off to work in a local Pub until eleven. It was a real team effort to keep going.

Another thing that happened was the boss's idea to go into Litho. This is a different form of printing which involved plate-making. Litho was eventually to take over from the letterpress which had been the way since Caxton's time. So the boss hired a man to join the firm as plate maker and machinist. The new machine was installed but the new operator reneged on the deal and left us in a fine mess.

Result: I got lumbered with the plate-making as well as my own work. Did I get a pay rise because of this? Did I hell! So I devised my own method of getting a pay rise.

Every year the Unions, who were very strong in those days, engineered a percentage deal. If they got five percent pay rise so did I, because I did the wages. If he noticed it Mr. Smith said nothing. If he had I would have said I was still a member of the Union.

Luck then played a part in my life and the Firm, Modern Press, was taken over by London Newspaper, South London Press. Mr. Smith left and I was in sole charge. My salary doubled and I was given a car and five gallons of petrol a week.

So life went on until the worst tragedy that can happen occurred: we lost our son, Paul, to a stupid car accident. Driving too fast into a bend Paul lost control and careered into a post. Not wearing a safety belt he was flung from the car which turned and ran over him, crushing his chest. His girlfriend who was wearing a belt survived, without a scratch.

Lots of couples would have broken up after this tragedy but Gwen and I clung together and managed to ride out the sadness.

Several years later the Firm went into liquidation and was no more. I eventually retired at sixty-seven; with any luck I will be ninety-one in April. Hallelujah!!

SOPHIE

Sleek and glossy as a seal, she was about ten months old. Sophie was a cross Labrador/Collie, black as the Ace of Spades. Sophie was not meant to be our dog but came to us anyway, and this is how it happened.

Paul had long wanted a dog but with Gwen and I both working, it was not a good idea. Paul however was not to be denied. He was then about ten-years-old and could read. Not that well but good enough to scan the local newspaper.

So I arrived home from work, dead beat as usual. Had my tea and settled down to have a look at the paper. The phone rang. Gwen answered it. Turning to me she said, 'There's some woman on here who wants to know when we are going to collect the dog.'

'Dog, dog,' I said, 'what dog?'

Paul, looking somewhat sheepish said, 'It was me, Dad.' Not good English, but I knew what he meant.

Well, Paul had picked up an ad in the local "rag", asking if anyone could give a good home to an unwanted dog.

'Better go and see what it's all about,' says Gwen as usual, devolving the responsibility to me.

Off Paul and I went to a house on the local Council Estate. Ten minutes later we arrived home complete with Sophie, a bowl, tin of dog food and the lead. I let the dog loose as soon as we were indoors and she flew into the sitting room, ran round, peed on the carpet and jumped into Gwen's lap. That was that!

We had a dog, or to be more correct, a bitch.

'You don't want a dog,' said Mother-in-law, but we kept her anyhow. Turned out to be probably the best non-investment we ever made.

First thing to do was to have Sophie spayed, for obvious reasons. Sophie was not impressed and when we brought her home she retreated to a corner of the lounge and sulked for days. However, she soon settled into family life and although Paul insisted she was his pet, inevitably she gravitated to the hand that fed her and walked her most of the time, Gwen.

Sophie soon established the pecking order. I was the boss and after a bit of training, she obeyed me instantly. Gwen was number two, giving due respect, because you don't bite the hand that feeds you. Not enough respect to obey her, however. Paul was treated as an equal, a sort of brother. Only Gwen and I were allowed to go near Sophie when she was feeding; Paul was warned off in no uncertain manner. Paul played with Sophie quite a lot when she was young, succeeding in breaking her tail. So for the rest of her life Sophie had a bent tail.

Between our bungalow and next door was a low wall and Sophie never attempted to jump over it. But things were about to change. New people, Rita and Mick, moved in and Sophie immediately went over the wall to make their acquaintance. This was the start of a lifelong friendship with Rita which earned Sophie the title "disloyal dog". We were able to go on holiday and leave Sophie with them. Once we did take her on holiday to the Norfolk Broads but it proved a disaster. In a hurry to get onto dry land she landed in the water and had to be rescued by a passing boatman, using a boat hook. Sophie spent the rest of the holiday curled on a bunk feeling very sorry for herself.

Sophie's one fault was that she was greedy and a thief as well. Not to mention crafty. Rita would sometimes give Sophie her dinner but when she came home she would bark at Gwen to tell her it was her dinner time. I have seen her take a sausage roll from the coffee table without breaking a stride.

We have many happy memories of Sophie, such as trampling through the woods, when Paul was young.

Age of course crept up on her and she suffered badly with arthritis and other ailments, so in the end the vet said it would be kinder to let her go. When the time came, as it does with all dogs and I had to take her to the Veterinary Surgery to be put down, it was a very sad day indeed. Paul who had left home by then was in tears, as was Gwen. But as I said we have so many happy memories of Sophie and we will never forget her.

CHILD MIGRANT

BY MICHAEL GORMLEY

I am a former child migrant, abandoned by my mother and placed in a convent at St. Anne's, Brighton at the age of two. From Brighton, probably at about age six, I was whizzed off to an orphanage called St. Mary's in Gravesend, Kent. My memories of England are mixed, some frightening and some quite pleasant. One day a Father Stinson visited the orphanage and asked me and the other boys if we would like to go to Australia. He said there was plenty of sunshine and we would ride ponies to school.

Of course I said, 'Yes.' Riding ponies to school!

I arrived in Freemantle, Western Australia, on the *SS New Australia* on 22nd February 1953. From Freemantle we were driven on the back of a truck to Clontarf Boys Town. On arrival the boys were split up into groups; one group went to Bindoon Orphanage and another group to Tardun Orphanage. It was a terribly sad and lonely experience; splitting us all up. I loved some of those boys and I would never see them again.

About the third day a group of us boys decided to flee our surroundings. We were walking along Manning Road and a truck pulled up beside us containing a Christian Brother who remarked, 'Where are you going, boys?'

I think we all responded, 'Perth, Brother.'

He drove us back to the orphanage without reprimanding us. I know one of the boys in the group was Colin Alexander. I don't know who the Brother was.

I spent eight-years in Clontarf and suffered terribly. My brain structure was altered as a result of the abuse – sexual, psychological and physical. Brother O'Shea was the Principal at the time and Brother Doyle, who was my primary caregiver, took the reins from 1953–1959. He taught me in my Junior Class; he was also the football coach. He was a hard taskmaster but I hold no animosity towards him or any of the other Brothers.

One day I was throwing rocks down the piggery. I was about nine and my elbow clicked. I imagined I badly bruised it, but felt too much fear and shame to report the incident. A couple of days later I was confronted by Brother Doyle. He noticed that I couldn't bend my arm. I was taken to the hospital and told I had chipped a bone in my elbow, but nothing would be done until I was older. A few years later on when I visited the hospital, they informed it could make the arm worse if they operated. So since the age of nine I have had an arm which I cannot straighten fully, with a bone sticking out of it. I was able to function alright with it; football, etc., albeit, at about seventy-percent capacity.

On another occasion I was up in the old vegetable tower looking at the graffiti on the wall. I heard footsteps on the stairwell below me and this dark figure appears before me; I froze with fear.

It was a Christian Brother.

'What are you doing up here (tower), Mick? Don't you know it's out of bounds?'

'Just looking at the writing on the wall, Brother,' I said fearfully.

His response was that I wait outside his room so he could come and deal with me. He dealt with me all right, by raping me. Later that night he came to my bed in the dormitory and asked me to go to confession. The sexual abuse affected me quite profoundly, following in the initial shock of the assault. I denied to myself that I had been assaulted.

I also made a promise to my abuser not to mention it to anyone. I imagine I tried to suppress the memory of what had happened in an attempt to regain my previous stability. I imagine I had shut down emotionally, which may have been a shock response to what happened to me.

Before the assault started the Christian Brother told me, he was going to show me 'what it was like.'

I imagined it was some sort of association with the graffiti I was perusing in the old vegetable tower. Part of me enjoyed the attention I received during the assault. Many years later I confronted my abuser and was able to express how I felt about the abuse he perpetrated upon me. He explained the hell he went through and the fear that one day I would confront him.

Later on I felt quite sad. He was a sad man who had his own demons to process. I have since forgiven him.

Apart from the abuse, I enjoyed the activities at Clontarf, namely, football, cricket and handball. We built the handball courts and every opportunity I had, I would play. There was one boy, Julian Gill, with whom I played quite a lot, but I could never beat him.

Every morning we would parade on the main quadrangle before scrambling off to school. In the winter months we played football on the quadrangle; a bunch of socks tied in a ball, which I really enjoyed. In the summer it would be cricket. Many of the boys used to keep pigeons – Wally Kerkoff comes to mind – and bantams.

Clontarf is situated on the Canning River and some of the boys used to go kyleing – a piece of metal shaped like a boomerang, which entailed throwing the kylie toward the front of the school of fish, hoping one would meet its maker. I tried it once, unsuccessfully. I know Hughie McConnell was quite adept.

Every year we would have a sports carnival – mini-Olympics. The boys were split up into four teams named after former Christian Brothers. Hefferans, Bodkins, Daleys and O'Connors, and after it was all over, most of us would be suffering from horrific sunburns. There was no awareness in those days of the dangers of the sun, and skin cancer.

I remember on the weekends, especially in the summer, kicking footballs, playing handball, sneaking out of the orphanage to buy cigarettes. I also remember the pain, the shame, the loneliness and not feeling I belonged. In retrospect, I had split off quite early; a defence mechanism against the terror that was locked in my body.

There were lots of other happenings at Clontarf which I don't think appropriate to list here. If anyone was brought up in a Boys Home, Orphanages, they would comprehend what I mean. A child needs to feel loved; a child needs to be cuddled.

I was kicked out of Clontarf late 1960 and spent the next forty years in another dimension, wandering aimlessly around Australia. I discovered alcohol, the magic elixir, which gave me temporary relief from the pain and fear which permeated my whole being. I couldn't stay in a job for very long. I've had over one hundred until I settled down and got married. I managed to stay in a government job for nine years. In the interim I discovered AA (Alcoholics Anonymous) where I met my ex wife, which curbed my drinking but wasn't effective in dealing with my demons.

Thirteen years ago I dropped into a black hole; four months of absolute terror. I wanted to end my life, but somehow I reached out to a friend who took me to hospital. I had three visits to the hospital in four months. I imagined I was in hell.

I imagine I was going through some sort of metamorphosis – mental, physical and spiritual. I had been in therapy since 1994, processing the terror, anxiety, annihilation from my childhood. My therapy consisted of one-to-one with a therapist, group work FOO (Family of Origin Therapy) and EMDR (Eye Movement Desensitization and Reprocessing).

I had a fear I would be locked away but the hospital nurses were very supportive. I didn't seem to have any control over my process. I was released from hospital 16th September 2004, but my anxiety had only subsided a little. One morning, waking up with my demons, I went down on my knees and asked Jesus Christ to have mercy on me and forgive me my sins. Over time my anxiety has dissipated and I believe (because I was prepared to face my demons) Jesus delivered me from my "psychological hell".

PHOTO ALBUM

Unbeaten 1937-38.

Group of St. Mary's boys.

John Flynn and Josie's wedding 1966.

Dave Millins' brother Harry on left, John Flynn centre foreground, and Ronnie Graham.

Irena Lyczkowska, John Flynn, Josie and Caroline 2013.

John Flynn's birthday with family.

Terry McKenna with Martha Glancy, birth mother.

Terry McKenna 2009 in Kent.

Terry McKenna with adoptive mother Kathleen 1985.

Mavis and Pat Heffernan with dog Tuppence.

Pat Heffernan with his beloved dog.

Antony and Gwen Hayman's wedding 1953.

Antony and Gwen Hayman at RAF Ball, Alhorn, Germany 1954.

Antony attending his garden, Kent.

Michael Gormley fourth from the right, holding up his work 1950s.

Michael Gormley, left, with friend, Clontarf Boys Home 1950s.

Michael Gormley, Philippines, 2012.

Antony Standen, Germany.

Rob and Sue Tyrell, Australia 1968.

"Bollerman," Mr. and Mrs. MacAuliffe.   *Colin Bedford.*

St. Mary's School, Gravesend

S.S. New Australia carried child migrants lured by false promises of sunshine, oranges and ponies.

KOKO EMAILS – 2016 & 2017

Pat,

Thanks for expanding on the various comments regarding the Pope's blessing to the Catholic Rescue Society on the occasion of the new home at Gravesend during 1925-1926. On another note you must be the only member of our group who does not know what "KOKO" means. It means Keep On Keeping On. It is a simple message of support to all our members as we are getting on in years. I can't imagine what happened to our exchange of emails, since all or most emails from me are "blind" copies to all the members.

Happy New Year to you and your carer.

KOKO (keep on keeping on), Pat.

(Delvin) John Flynn

John,

In response to you, re Pat being the only member who questions the meaning of KOKO, if he reads "The Boys of St. Mary's" the group's philosophy runs throughout the book in all their emails and stories. To me KOKO signifies the effort to handle life the way it has been put to us, also it encourages us with a unique motto; simply keep on keeping on when, in some circumstances, we want to give up rather than deal with the problem at hand. The pastor living in my building has read "Boys" and finds the stories remarkable. Each time we meet he responds with a

"KOKO" and said the letters remind him to do exactly what they convey. We are touching not only the lives of our members but those who have no connection to our group.

KOKO.

With affection.

Caroline

FOOLISH THOUGHTS FOR THE DAY/ CHEERFUL LAUGH

From Ann.

Chance would be a fine thing... Stay sharp... Live Life... Love life...

Regards,

Ann

SEX AT 73...

I just took a leaflet out of my mail box informing me I can have sex at 73. I'm so happy because I live at 89 and it's not too far to walk home afterwards. And it's the same side of the street. I don't even have to cross the road.

Answering Machine Message: 'I am not available right now but thank you for caring to call. I'm making changes in my life. Please leave a message after the beep. If I don't return your call you're one of the changes.'

'My wife and I had words but I didn't get to use mine.'

'Frustration is trying to find your glasses without your glasses.'

'Blessed are those who can give without remembering and take without forgetting.'

'The irony of life is, by the time you're old enough to know your way round, you're not going anywhere.'

'God made man before woman so as to give him time to think of an answer for her first question.'

'I was always taught to respect my elders but it keeps getting harder to find one.'

'Every morning is the dawn of a new error.'

'Aspire to inspire before you expire.'

Hi John,

Not sure if it is your end or mine but messages are not coming through.

Is this a New Year's spirit playing tricks on us?

Hope all is well.

L & H's.

Caroline

To All:

I hope you managed to see a beautiful picture of Caroline, the author of our book.

KOKO.

Josie and John

John,

One word. Thanks!

As always you are too kind with your compliments and I know I will have to live up to them.

Sincere thanks for sending the picture to our "family".

Caroline

John/Colin,

Thank you for your kind comments re: the picture taken when reaching the big Nine-O. Although one cannot judge an image on paper it is good to put a face to a person, long connected to our group of writers, worldwide.

My appreciation to John for making this possible.

KOKO.

Caroline

John,

An amazing person who until now has only been a name. Thanks, John, for Caroline's picture. We will keep it on our KOKO collection record.

Love and best wishes for the New Year to you and Josie.

Colin and Eileen

CANADA

Happy New Year all, from an Old St. Mary's Boy here in Ayr, Ontario.

Roy Daniels

John,

Feedback on the 90th birthday picture is overwhelming; one I never expected. As mentioned by Colin and Eileen the name connected to "The Boys" now has a face. I am delighted to know they will store the picture you sent in their KOKO collection and continue to stay within this remarkable "family".

Did our Leader have this insight to camaraderie when he set up the group in 1988?

L & H's.

Caroline

John,

A very nice picture of Caroline. She looks very Royal.

KOKO.

Michael Monaghan

John,

With all your latest practising, John, you could be the new David Bailey!

Terry McK…

Response:

Is he one of our St. Mary's boys, Terry?

KOKO.

John

Eileen and Colin

This is not the first book published by Caroline. She has written about her time at St. Anne's orphanage located in Orpington, also of meeting her brother Rowland for the first time when he was in his seventies and he then travelled to Canada to live the last very happy remaining years of his life with her.

KOKO.

John

John,

Firstly, thank you for advising Colin and Eileen of "Surviving The Shadows" released in 2009, with the sequels of "Rowland: A Heart of Sunshine" in 2011 and "Under The Old Railway Clock" in 2014 about brother William, who was also at St. Mary's from the age of three to sixteen when he was sent to Bletchingly to work on the Farm. I am sorry these books were not published while both my brothers were still alive as I know they would have been thrilled at the idea of "telling all", which was constantly on their minds, plus the humour of their Navy experience.

Look after yourself.

With hugs and love to you and Josie.

KOKO.

Caroline

Letter to John, dated January 11, 2016

Dear Mr. Flynn,

I hope you don't mind me contacting you. I am Louise (Smith) and you have been speaking to my sister Barbara Knight about our father Mr. Smith who you knew from your days at St. Mary's in Gravesend.

As you know my sister has been unwell for several years and her condition has become much worse lately. It's with this in mind that I thought I would make contact with you. I have bought your book and begun to learn how hard life must have been for all you boys. I found it very moving and I can't imagine what life must have been like for all of you. Could you clarify my father's position there?

I was born at Glen View in April 1954, which I think was just before you left the Orphanage. I was led to believe I was named after a Nun at St. Mary's; did you know of her? Incidentally, I always felt blessed I look like my mother whom as you rightly remember, was a shy lady. But my personality is very similar to my father's – rather than the other way round. I understand from Barbara that you have fond memories of my father which I'm pleased about. As in the book most of the boys memories about him seem to be about him disciplining them; at times it would seem unfairly.

My dad spoke about the Nuns being very much in charge of the orphanage. Part of his responsibility was to discipline the boys on their command! I understand he was unhappy about this and he often challenged them when he felt this was unjustified. I was always told this was the main reason he left St. Mary's. I expect you knew this from Barbara. My father died in May 1966 when my children were in their teens and he is still missed by us all. My three children and his other five grandchildren absolutely doted on him as did my siblings. His legacy lives on today; my daughter having been taught by him to box when she was a very small girl. She became a personal trainer which is the equivalent of being a P.T. Instructor.

Your book will form part of their memories of him (and their children too) in future years. So I just want you to know that it will always be valued as part of their heritage. Personally I remember him as a man with a huge capacity to love (especially children) and an inner confidence to live life as he chose. An unfailing sense of humour and a love of learning, barley wine and snazzy shirts. I genuinely felt privileged to have had him as my father and still miss him so much every day.

Warmest regards,

Louise Simmonds.

Acknowledgement:

Dated January 12, 2016

Dear Louise,

So delighted that you took the trouble to write. Your father was my hero and mentor. I truly regret I was never to see him again after I left St. Mary's in Sept. 1954. I found my mother and other members of my family. Notwithstanding that they didn't want to be found. But how do you trace a man named Smith? I was speaking to your sister Barbara over the Christmas period and like her mother, I think she is shy and her memories are not so easily forthcoming. I remember her as a child being very withdrawn. This is evidenced by the school photo she sent me. She appears in the photo as though she didn't want to be noticed. It was a very nice experience to be present at your family gatherings at Glen View and to observe your father in an entirely different role as a parent, as opposed to a housemaster.

I remember you as a tiny baby and your brother. You could easily been named after Sister Louise who was the most popular Nun at St. Mary's. I kept in touch with her until she died. Another popular Nun was Sister Magdalen. I admired your dad immensely. He had style and panache. I mimicked everything about him – his clothes (when I was old enough to buy my own), his posture. Everything. His views made a deep impression on me. We never knew the likes of him before or after. He was a great communicator.

If you ever feel inclined to talk about your father I could expand on what I have written here.

Best wishes and to quote our group's motto: KOKO.

Keep On Keeping On.

(Delvin) John Flynn

Connection to St. Mary's

Hi Louise,

My name is Terry McKenna and a member of the former "inmates" of St. Mary's in Gravesend who send emails via "Delvin" a.k.a. John Flynn. The book is really down to two members of our little group of friends from around the world. John started it all in 1988 I believe, at a suggestion from someone at what was originally called The Catholic Children's Rescue Society which started some 125 years ago and based in Southwark, London. I am not too sure John knew of the road he was going down on, some 28 years ago. And what a journey he has and still is having on all our behalf.

Over the years the CRS, later renamed Cabrini in 2008 and with whom John has formed a brilliant relationship, so many of our group have benefit from his genuine concern and charming "Irish" ways and established a friendship we all enjoy. It was those emails he diligently kept for years which gave Caroline Whitehead, the book's author, and herself a former resident at St. Anne's in Orpington, run by a similar order of Nuns as St. Mary's.

Sadly a few years ago John suffered a break-in at his home and among the many valuables taken was his personal computer. He hadn't saved anything and thinking now that all was "lost". Although a relative newcomer to the group of about six years I had kept a lot of emails because I too was thinking of writing my own story and all it entailed, and I thought these emails might be a great help in my own research. As a result I now get all emails from John (except personal ones) and became his backup system. So all was not lost!

I have enjoyed many visit to Chez Flynn, where John and his wife Josie are so welcoming. I hope to go again very soon. Between us I managed to collate all our various emails and brought them back home to Bristol. It took me quite some time to put them into a form of order but was so worth it. Caroline came over for a visit in 2013 to see John and several long-standing friends. At that time I'd never met John nor Caroline, and this was a good time to do so. And I did, and haven't looked back since. Caroline who was 90 last year is an author of distinction. You may want to take a look on Amazon at her books. They are: "Rowland A Heart of Sunshine", "Surviving The Shadows" and her latest "Under The Old

Railway Clock". Well worth a look and very well written. It was Caroline who was able to get my own story published through her publisher, in what seemed like no time at all. I have sent you a copy of my book, some of which is featured in "The Boys of St. Mary's".

Due to her resilience and amazing determination Caroline eventually got OUR book into print. I had the pleasure of staying with Caroline at her home in British Columbia in April/May last year for six weeks, when the "proof" reading came to her for final edit before going off to the printers. I had a great time and this mere "stripling" of then sixty-six was regally looked after by Caroline.

Not sure if you know what KOKO means as we sign off. It means Keep On Keeping On and has become our motto.

Yours most sincerely,

KOKO.

Terry McKenna

Sequel to "Boys"

Hi Terry,

Have just finished asking John to send you a copy of Louise's email regarding the book and the Mr. Smith mentioned in it was her father. Life is indeed a small world; the fact she was able to get and buy the book is a tribute to not only her father, our group, but her children too and the heritage of future generations. I wonder what prompted her in the first place to hear the group had published their memories of St. Mary's, along with their personal stories such as your own, your brother Michael, Ron Mulligan, Antony Hayman and John Michael Murray, along with John's excellent and meaningful introduction to the book.

With all that is coming out of the woodwork, and providing John approves the next step, I feel Terry we should tackle the next project of a sequel to "Boys". It is selling well and its capacity is giving us more insight to those who were either at St. Mary's or connected, like Louise's father Mr. Smith, who appeared a man of integrity and did not wish to unduly chastise unruly boys as the regime demanded of him.

Having previously discussed my crummy computer, while it still functions,

I must admit my latest manuscript "Leggy Tales" – no, not about unruly Catholic boys and girls, has disappeared totally after finishing, editing and ready for the publisher. Even Don can't find it. So, Terry, it looks as though your technical expertise even with this machine would possibly work if you can fathom the next move?

Your message to Louise says it all. It is with sincere hope she and her family read "The Boys of St. Mary's" and while understanding where her good father came from, she will also understand the reason why those brought up at the school need to voice their memories of childhood. I believe Mr. Smith was well thought of. One curious note: Louise's statement she was named after a Nun. The Nuns at St. Mary's were the Sisters of Charity while the St. Anne's Nuns were the Sisters of Mercy; inappropriately named when you realize the story of their strict upbringing of the girls under their care which unfolds in "Surviving The Shadows".

At all times, Terry, your recording of information and details of events continues to be much appreciated by everyone. My very sincere thanks for all your help now, and over the past year, when negotiating the safety of OUR personal records with the new owners of OUR files at Chatham.

Hope you are coping, pain-wise. No doubt, you chuckled with our latest health news. Indeed – falling apart!

Yes, we keep on keeping on, thanks to John who took us on this journey back in 1988, in the first place.

With hugs.

Caroline

Bald Eagles

Caroline and Ann,

Knowing Caroline she will really have appreciated that magnificent picture of the eagle. When I visited her some years ago she pointed out the beauty of the landscape and the wealth of wildlife. Sadly I was not as knowledgeable as her and much of what she talked about passed me by. One particular instance I recall was when Caroline spotted a Bald Eagle high, high on a tall tree. I think she said it was a Redwood tree. I looked but still could not see it. I think in the end I just pretended. Caroline loves the wild open countryside and she pointed out a little known fact that although the Bald Eagle is the national emblem of the USA, there are more Bald Eagles in Canada. I wondered if it could be attributed to the NRA (the Gun Lobby) justifying the deaths caused by their unholy sales? But that is another story.

Keep sending the lovely picture and stories, Ann.

Love. KOKO

John

Man and Bird

Hi Ann,

An incredible story of man and bird. Knowing the intelligence of eagles it did not surprise me how both were capable of helping each other, in time of need.

As a point of interest in "Leggy Tales", a manuscript not quite ready for the publisher, in the chapter "Crafty Crows" I recall eagles flying across the ocean to their territory. Despite the noise and aggravating behaviour of a dozen or more crows who were bent on distracting its flight, the eagle appeared not in the least stressed as it meandered on without causing injury or harm. With one swipe of its large wing an eagle could "down" a crow in seconds. But eagles are not killers unless searching for food. It seems with their telepathic senses, when invading another bird's territory, they are aware other birds need to survive.

Thanks to Ray Hawkins for sending this compassionate experience of man and bird.

With love.

Caroline

Evacuation

Tony,

I enjoyed our chat yesterday.

Ron Mulligan's evocative account of his and other children's movements tells us so much. Ron writes: September 3 1939. Who can ever forget that date? The day World War Two was declared on Germany. But on Sunday morning the boys of St. Mary's Children's Home, Gravesend, Kent, had other things on their minds: "Evacuation". The entire school, all of two hundred boys, eleven Nuns (Sisters of Charity) were being sent to the countryside for safety from the expected air raids. We arrived at Gravesend Dock and boarded the pleasure boat Royal Daffodil and set sail down the Thames and headed for the North Sea. We arrived at the Port of Lowestoft in the country of Suffolk. The boys were split up, and Ron was picked to stay with four other boys who were driven in a chauffeur car to a large stately home called Reddisham Hall Estate. You can read a full riveting account of Ron's story starting on Page 101 in the book of "The Boys of St. Mary's", by Caroline Whitehead.

After various escapades Ron was moved on to Ugbrooke House, stately home of Lord and Lady Clifford near Chudleigh in Exeter. Ron left Ugbrooke in 1943, whilst the rest of us stayed until the end of the War in 1945. But the question you asked Tony was when did we all travel to Chudleigh?

Like me, you were sent like a parcel from one place to another. I was staying variously at a nursery at Streatham, London, or Salisbury or Foxhill or West Haddon or Rugby. According to the records given to me, at some point in 1942 we were transferred to Chudleigh; that is if you were not already there. So after all that I've not been able to determine what date the bulk of the boys were transferred, because of the boys being split up at the outbreak of the War. This may explain the vagueness of the dates. Perhaps Colin Bedford may come back to us with more information. One thing that is clear at the end of 1945 we were all labelled and returned to St. Mary's in Gravesend.

Sorry I have not been more helpful, Tony.

KOKO from Josie and John.

PS/

In Antony Hayman's adventures starting on page 7, he mentions on page 13 the boys were transferred to Ugbrooke by February 1941.

PPS/

The boys' personal accounts are all very interesting and worth reading again. I know when I go back to them their stories are so refreshing. It is like reading them for the first time.

World War two

The beginning of WW2 must have been a bit of a shock to the Nuns with 200 boys to take care of and to ensure an orderly evacuation from the building and area. But their care did not end with that. As they had to care and oversee where their charges were and probably keep tabs on them until the prospect of their return. "Their", of course, being us!

I wonder what the Nuns' reactions would be to the "Boys" book?

Michael M

Dogfights

Hi John,

Speaking of WW2, I imagine the Nuns everywhere were as devastated as the children in their care when War broke out and fervently prayed all of them would be returned safely to their schools, when hostilities ceased.

As you know, Orpington is close to Biggin Hill Aerodrome where many of the air fights took place and was heavily bombed. I remember well the dogfights and the heavy shrapnel we found in the playground and were not allowed to keep, but had to hand it over to a Nun. When the sirens began to wail it was not the girls who panicked. It was the Nuns in their black habits flying here, there and everywhere hoping all tiny hands and feet were in the Crypt below the church, to ensure the children's safety. We mumbled hymns and prayers amid the noise in the sky as we huddled on bunk beds, hoping to stay there for ever. But of course it was not to be. To hope for a slice of bread and jam while all this fighting was going on in the skies above was a treat we wished for, but never got. As soon as the all-clear sounded the Nuns panicked again to check to see what damage had been done by the heavy bombing.

When the Infirmary and the Laundry were blown to pieces, one Nun said with the utmost philosophy. 'It was the Will of the Lord.' The Church standing close by, stood untouched; not one brick was damaged.

A number of St. Anne's girls joined the Army and came back to the school in uniforms. May Lyle could not get her Brownie camera out fast enough. I believe she was more proud of the uniform than the girl wearing it.

Late to have regrets but it would have been of much help had the girls an inkling of life beyond the Orphanage walls, to avoid the many pitfalls they encountered when wearing a uniform. One "old" girl from St. Anne's wore the uniform of the Land Army. In all her innocence where she worked at the first farm she appeared meek and mild, and it was not until she experienced the farmer's technique with young girls did it cause her to request a move to another farm, with a pronged fork in mind, should she encountered the same experience.

So many stories are still out there with humour and compassion, which leaves me in awe of how we coped with life without the help from family.

Take care.

KOKO.

Caroline

Inquirer

What was all this about the War? Someone was telling me about the evacuation during the outbreak of war.

And who is Tony? And Ron? I don't understand.

Help!

Signed Eileen (Chase)

Eileen,

A bunch of us boys born in the thirties and forties were brought up in an Orphanage and we collaborated in the writing of a book by Caroline Whitehead who herself grew up in an orphanage. Over number of years some of our members of a writing group worldwide, have written their account of what it was like and Caroline got the book published, which has included these stories and several emails sent between us, covering many years. The book can be obtained from Amazon under the title "The

Boys of St. Mary's". ISBN 978-1-927755-23-5. All books published are under their own number.

This is also available on Ebooks on Kindle.

By the way you are making spectacular progress with your own writing and using the computer.

John

War History

Hello John,

Yes, it is Saturday morning and normally I don't respond to the computer as it is catch-up time with cleaning and other chores of the week. However, I value my special friends without whose input the KOKO group worldwide would never have existed.

The message from Eileen tells me she was not born before or during the era of disruption of the War and does not appear cognitive of its history. After sending her details of how to obtain a copy of "Boys", perhaps she would be curious enough to buy OUR book.

Take care John and Josie.

Caroline

Down Under

Hello John and Josie,

This email is to bring you up-to-date on how we are sailing here, Down Under. Yesterday Mavis and I celebrated our 25th wedding anniversary, legal years, plus 12 years practice. Young Mavis's health is reasonably good. On the other hand, I keep hitting brick walls. My lungs have caused constant visits to doctors and a lung specialist. I visit the specialist every 3 to 6 months. My lung condition is pleural plaque, caused by exposure to Asbestos when I was in the Navy. I cough a lot and often get short of breath. I recently had yet another CAT scan and a lung test, where I breathe into a machine connected to a computer. The chap who designed and built the machine must have been a devotee of The Marquis de Sade. Nothing much can be done, other than attempting to reduce damage to my lungs with medication and puffers. I am too old for a lung transplant. Please do not believe for one minute that I am seeking sympathy. I am not. I have accepted my condition. I do not hold any grudge against the Royal Navy using Asbestos in their warships and submarines during my term of service.

Mavis and I carry on with life enjoying ourselves. Later this year, in September, we will be taking a cruise of the Barrier Reef aboard The Pacific Aria (P & O ship) along with 250 former submariners from around Australia. The National AGM of the Australian Association will be held at sea.

Should all go well with my health we are considering a short visit to England next year. We are playing it by ear. For years, as a young chap, I hardly needed to see a doctor. Now I am unable to keep away from them. Two weeks ago I had my fifth small skin cancer removed. It has been two from my right leg, one from my left leg, one from my right wrist and one from my right ear. I'm now having problems with my left ear, which was operated on by a Royal Naval Surgeon back in 1963 at the Plymouth Naval Hospital, HMS Drake. I now need a special CAT scan. It has all come about by my losing my balance and tests show I have a build up of fluid at the rear of my ear.

Incidentally, if you take a close look at me in one or two of the photos in the 2016 Calendar we sent you, you will notice I have lost a bit of weight – over a stone and a half in one year. I have always been a "Mr. Puniverse" or "Hercules Untrained". Now look at it! Don't worry, we are both making the most of life. Last week we attended the Royal Edinburgh Military Tattoo. It visited Melbourne (only its 4th time held outside of Scotland). It was a wonderful performance. In the next few weeks we will be attending John Cleese and Eric Idle's world show. Our only downside is that Mavis's son Matthew and his wife have separated. Their children have chosen to live with him and he is coping very well.

We hope you and Josie are both well. Will you be moving from your home or staying where you are?

Love.

Pat and Mavis

Cliche

As a young boy just starting work, I asked my English teacher at Night School if he could give me one hint about good writing. He said: 'In a nutshell, avoid cliches like the plague!'

KOKO, if it has not become a cliche.

John

Keep them coming

Hello you ALL,

Please keep the emails a-coming. Loving them all.

XX,

Ann

Sunday Morn: 7am

John,

It is Sunday 7am, normally a time I decide to leave the technological world over the weekend, to catch up on other chores. In your message no doubt you said it all, covering Paddy's health condition. I empathize with him his ongoing struggles to KOKO. But, as our motto aptly puts these words in a nutshell, while we understand the effort to do so with much more endurance, being who we are, we know we will never give up but continue to KOKO. It is one thing for Paddy to be suffering the way he is, but of course we all feel for him and hope he can enjoy some quality of life, however small.

To Mavis and Paddy, congratulations from this part of the globe on your 25th wedding anniversary. My best wishes to future years of well-being and happiness.

Your comment, John, rings true when you look back at childhood days to realize its effect on just what an institutionalized upbringing does, and at some point down the road rear its head. With these disabilities, as we age in years, shows the stuff we are made of as we continue with life in the best way possible. Susan Tananbaum, our friendly Professor of Social History, Brunswick, US, introduced to me by you John some years ago when you two met in London, continues to be of interest in collecting the history of Catholic Homes and is currently working on another article which I hope, when completed, she will forward copy. You know from recent messages she bought a copy of "The Boys of St. Mary's" and said she was reading and enjoying the interesting stories and emails from our group of writers. No doubt, with Susan's open mind she will grasp the situation; the humour and pathos in these old boys' memoirs. As you rightly put it, had these times not been recorded while we are all compos mentis, imagine the enormous loss of our heritage.

Your humour, despite your daily overload, continues to amaze me. My total admiration goes to you in bucket loads. The thought of living another twenty years or so is awe-inspiring, to say the least. Although I constantly chide myself age is but a number, the reality does hit one between the already missing tooth since reaching the big nine-O, other parts of deterioration surely to follow. But you know, John, the tenacity of our group is we soldier on, regardless. I loved Margaret Thatcher's comment: 'No such thing as society.' With finance and constantly propping up those I love, it leaves an irreparable hole in already frayed pockets. It appears I am not alone.

Hope all is well with you and Josie.

KOKO. With love.

Caroline

Diagrama

Dear Nathan,

It is my understanding Ian Forbes is no longer with Diagrama. At the meeting of February 2015 between John Flynn (at his home), Terry McKenna, Ian Forbes, Elaine Brewster, it was determined at this meeting that Ian Forbes would be the contact person with whom to get in touch if any of our group members, whose records you currently hold either at Purley or Chatham, required to inspect their files. So far Diagrama have not had the courtesy to advise (Delvin) John Flynn or Terry McKenna of the person now in charge or a telephone number as a point of contact. In our negotiations with Diagrama and Cabrini we were assured of transparency, access to our records, and also Ian Forbes committed to

Terry McKenna he would get back to him with the details of this person and who in turn would forward them on to (Delvin) John Flynn. Thus far, as we are left in the dark I am requesting your urgent assistance in providing our group in London with the appropriate information.

Many thanks.

Caroline (Canada, group member)

Birthday Wishes

Terry,

Have a great 67th birthday today, May 12, 2016.

Best Wishes. KOKO.

Josie and John

Choice

Ooooooh John,

Only another two days for your birthday too. Are you excited to see what Josie has bought you or maybe going to treat you to a lovely breakfast in your "New" local greasy spoon? Or a lunch at the local pub?

I read from your emails that you have plenty of choice.

KOKO and Hi to Josie.

Michael M

dated: 15 May, 2016.

Skyped Chat

Hi John,

Just noticed the time of your email was 05:36! Still I suppose it is light and allows you time to yourself which must be precious to you these days. Well, I am off to see a certain Brian Wilson and Al Jardine both original members of the famed "Beach Boys" at the Colston Hall in Bristol tonight and so looking forward to it.

I received an email from Antony Hayman saying he too had been emailed by Don Boston, Caroline's son-in-law. One assumes that no news is good news as far as her present state of health is concerned.

I had a lovely day in Dorset with her friend Marion "celebrating" my birthday on Thursday. At eighty (hers not mine) she is still full of fun. She has just bought herself an iPad but hadn't got WI-FI in her flat but it is available in the communal lounge. Sound familiar? Anyway, I arranged for her to get a Broadband connection, which I think will happen one day next week. BT take note of the speed this can be done. A former classmate from my primary school days at St. Francis RC School in Maidstone yesterday Skyped me and we had a lengthy chat (both ways honest) which was very nice.

Are you celebrating your birthday on Tuesday or just chilling out at home? Whatever you do I hope you have the lovely day you so deserve and get a chance to enjoy yourself.

So happy 77th on the 17 May, so to speak.

KOKO as ever and regards to Josie.

Terry McK...

Fifty-Odd Years

Terry,

You have got the measure of my situation. After fifty odd years of Josie looking after me, the baton has been passed on to me and it's my turn to look after her. It's not easy. Whilst I run fast as I can, I do my best to cover all the tasks Josie used to do. On health and safety grounds she is banned from the kitchen and chafes at not being able to do all these things. But as you know we have to let go at sometime in our lives.

I hope Caroline is progressing well, as you do too. And so enjoy your concert. Your love of music makes me realize for some of the wrong reasons I have missed some of the finer times of my teenage years. So I say thank you for introducing me to music like the ELO, which I have now started to listen to. I feel I have been a victim of "music snobbery". If snobbery wasn't so funny it would be cruel. Remember John Cleese and the other two (it was Ronnie Barker and Ronnie Corbett) I looked down on him because I am upper class. 'I know my place.'

KOKO.

John

Birthday Wishes

John,

Happy birthday today. I'd forgotten how young you are but good you are able to measure up to the extra calls on you in doing more of the household chores Josie has had to relinquish. But you have had plenty of experience in your younger days under the direction of Mrs. Grundle and more gentle tasks under the direction of Sister Joseph in the sacristy. This early start must have built up your strength and stamina for latter day responsibilities.

I have been enjoying reading the accounts of some of the boys about their days at St. Mary's and after. They prove to be compelling reading amid a mixture of emotions. I would heartily recommend any who have not got a copy to get one and have it ready on a "rainy day".

Happy birthday, John, and happy days to all our readers.

Happy days to Josie too in the new adventure of Sidcup Hill and about.

KOKO.

Michael M

Thanks!

Terry,

Just to thank you and all for your good wishes.

KOKO.

John

Back on Line

Hi Caroline,

Just a quick hello from all your friends in the UK. We are all hoping things have improved with you and you are making a good recovery and back at home or at least with family, Caroline jnr. and Don. Several members of our group have naturally sent their very best.

Ann is now back on line and I re-sent her your email address because I believe she has been having problems with her computer. Who hasn't, I ask?

I have loaded two photos from John Flynn's recent 77th birthday celebrations. One with his cake and two with his children and Josie. Lastly, Marion was on top form when I saw her on my own birthday on the 12th and I do believe she too is back on line, so you may get an email some time soon; do look out!

Tony Hayman as ever sends his fondest wishes and from all of us KOKO. I know Don will look after you as he also does.

Regards.

Hope to hear from you soon.

KOKO.

Terry McK…

As We Age

Hi Terry,

Came out of hospital Wednesday and now staying with Caroline jnr. and Don until mid-June, when Don returns from his home after visiting family in Sudbury, Ontario.

Life will be at a slower pace and I am not sure if I will be able to cope with the adjustment to a once very energetic lifestyle. Truly, at this time, I find it a little depressing with the possibility drugs will now play a large role in my mental outlook.

Sorry to have missed both yours and John's birthdays. Such is life, as we age.

The picture of John and Josie cheered me greatly.

Will be in touch soon.

With hugs.

Caroline

Great News

Hi Caroline,

Great news that you are at least out of the hospital and are with Caroline jnr. whilst Don is visiting his family in Ontario. I forwarded your email to John and Ann Phyall to let them know the good news too. I am guessing you won't like taking any medication I assume you are now on, but it seems it is necessary. I hope you can take in some of the lovely weather that I so enjoyed last year, when visiting.

Am off tomorrow to Eastbourne for a couple of days chairing a panel review board case between a Tenant and my Housing Association; something I have done for some three years now or so. It is 200 miles from Bristol to Eastbourne (West Coast to East Coast) and I will stay at a hotel on Monday and drive back home on Tuesday after the hearing. I might call in on Marion on the way home, so I can return her cake container and board from the cake surprise, surprise she baked for me. I was able to blow out the candles this time, unlike when you and I visited her in 2013. I just hope she is in (you know her). If not, I will leave it with the concierge at the residence and I know she will pass it on.

Have a pile of ironing to do today, so will listen to my music as I do it. I went to my second "Pop" show concert in six weeks last Sunday to see the amazing Brian Wilson of the Beach Boys famed group and original member Al Jardine in Bristol and it was brilliant. Wilson's song writing stands the test of time that's for sure.

Regarding my "delightful" sister I am now waiting for a date and time when I can go and do the DNA swab test that she has now said she will accept whatever the outcome! This is I believe because her lovely daughter, my niece Vanessa's common sense approach to her mother's disgraceful and self-centred attitude recently, you know about. When it comes back that we share the same mother I am not too sure what will happen or may be I am. It will take a lot of apologies from my sister Louise to restart our relationship again, if ever! Her entire attitude in recent weeks has been so distasteful and so unexpected as well as self-motivated with absolutely no consideration or thought given to OUR mother; herself in the throes of an increasing dementia problem which is hard for me to see, after all my efforts to find her and the almost sixty-years it took. Or, of course, my own feelings too. Trouble is I don't want to cut my nose off to spite my face (what a funny saying it is), so I may have to bite my tongue, or not. I am usually a forgiving soul and do not hold grudges ever. But I do not like to be messed around one little bit either, nor will I accept sheer ignorance and bullying tactics. I am true to my star sign of Taurus; stubbornness. We will see.

Once again so glad you are more or less back home where you belong and I wish you a speedy and full recovery. Stay well and healthy.

KOKO,

Terry McK…

Test Match

Hi John, Josie and Ann,

Have forwarded an email from Caroline I have just received. So pleased she is at Don and daughter Caroline's and is out of hospital. I know just how much she hates any form of medication but maybe realizes she now has to depend on them a little more to assist her, probably for the rest of her life. We all know she is not like that one bit; not the help, but the potential loss of some of her freedom she rightly values so much. At least at the moment she is in a better place than she was and back on her computer, though how often I am not too sure. I don't know anyone who deserves our thoughts more than Caroline does and we hope she recovers her fantastic zest for life. You John and Josie have been such good and valued friends to her for so many years, much longer than this "young pup"! She does grow on you, doesn't she, and we know why.

Am off myself to Eastbourne chairing a panel review board on Monday and Tuesday between a Tenant and my Housing Association. Not been to Eastbourne in years. I wonder if it is in colour these days?

Have a pile of ironing to do so will watch the Great North Run on BBC 2, as I do it. The Test Match finished in under three days again, and will listen to my music as I do most days.

Let's hope our friend Caroline gets so much better in the near future. One thing I know it will not be for the lack of Keep On Keeping On!

Terry

Learning Process

'morning John,

It is as you can imagine, a learning process in healing both in mind and body since my heart attack. At this time I am struggling to recognize that life is not going to be as it was, but at snail's pace. Still all could have been so much worse, despite a reaction after the Angiogram procedure when it appeared a vein had been nicked, causing my right arm to fill with blood; the result of which took two hours at the Jubilee Hospital to control and left me with a huge bruise from the wrist down beyond my elbow. Oxygen was depressed from the wrist and the swelling caused by this has only just returned to normal.

This machine does not perform with the slightest touch, but I wanted to ask how you and Josie are settling in your new home at Sidcup? Hope all is good with the move and you will soon make new friends.

Bruce has not given me the last quarter sales for "Boys" but when he does I will let you know.

Keep well and happy.

Much love and hugs.

Caroline

Health Service

Caroline,

It is good to learn that you are receiving the best of care. You have always given glowing reports of the Canadian health service and now it is your turn to benefit and get back to good health. It is tough for someone like you who has always enjoyed bags of energy but I can think of no one who is more up to the challenge and has the strength of character to overcome your present set-back.

Ours is a lovely apartment with heaps of space except for storage, and the shops are just a short walk away. Josie has already made new friends with some of the residents. For some reason I have lost a lot of weight and I am not impressed with our medical centre here at Sidcup. Firstly, I had to register for the both of us, then we made an appointment which was used up copying our medication list. When that finished I thought we would touch on why we had visited – but no. The doctor said his allocated time was ten minutes and we have to arrange yet another appointment after we have the results of blood tests.

KOKO.

Love.

John

New Residence

Caroline,

I am confident knowing you as I do, you will recover your normal energy and before long be back to your former self. Just KOKO.

This is a lovely place as Terry will affirm but is not a cheap option. So long as we can manage the outgoings, the future looks bright.

Our address is: 42 Kingswood Court, 47/51 Sidcup Hill, Sidcup, Kent, DA14 6FH.

KOKO and love.

John and Josie

Dummies

Michael,

Thank you for your kind thoughts and the pictures of the old place (St. Mary's). It was a bad day when they knocked it down – vandalism on a grand scale. If it still existed today it would be a "Listed" building. The quality of the fixtures and fittings – door handles, locks etc. would fetch a fortune today, not to mention those beautiful panel doors. Can you remember when the men were laying down the new lino? The lino must have been a quarter of an inch thick.

That stuff was never going to wear out. Remember polishing the lino with "Dummies", with some of our number sitting on them for a free ride and others skating with the blanket pieces tied to our feet.

Michael, you have gone and done it now! Dredging up those old memories.

KOKO.

John

Picture Postcard

Ha, h, ha,

"Dredging up those old memories". It will take your mind off some of the little disappointments at your otherwise ideal new home. I sent away to America for that picture postcard some time ago. I thought I had sent it to you. But I found it again under the settee. The card was sent by a resident to her mother when St. Mary's was Milton Mount College in 1930 for two and a half penny stamps. Note the tennis courts on the lawn in front of the grand building. Hope you still have an album of old Gravesend views; some feature Echo Square and views of St. Mary's from Parrock Road, Echo Square and the entrance gates.

Have a lovely day today on Sidcup Hill and the area round and about.

KOKO to all and of course you and Josie.

Michael M

Red Wax Polish

Hello John,

The message from Michael was most interesting and especially for him to remember the building of St. Mary's so well. You talk about half an inch of lino installed on the floors; today's quality perhaps of Oriental manufacture, would not last five minutes with the polishing machines we used in those days.

But didn't the floors shine, like the stars, especially after the St. Anne's girls had gone down on their knees to splash the red wax on them, stand back and admire their work. The fitting installed in all the Homes in the earlier days, yes, if sold, they would have been worth a small fortune.

Hope all is well in your new home and you are finding time for yourself.

Keep well. KOKO.

My love and hugs.

Caroline

May Day Morn'

Hello John, Hello Josie, Hello All,

I'm up and about early and enjoying thoroughly all the jokes again, mainly from Ann. It has been on my mind for a while thinking if John sings Josie a song now they live on Sidcup Hill. It resembles the song of a lass who lived on Richmond Hill.

On Sidcup Hill there lived a lass more bright than Mayday Morn'

Who charms all other maids surpass a rose, and me a thorn

This lass so neat, with smiles so sweet

Has won my right good will

I'd proud resign to call her mine

Sweet lass on Sidcup Hill.

Sweet lass on Sidcup Hill

Sweet lass on Sidcup Hill

I'm proud to resign and and call thee mine

Sweet lass on Sidcup Hill.

God speed to John and Josie on Sidcup Hill.

KOKO.

Michael M

Brand New

Hi Michael and one and all,

As usual I did things slightly different from the rest of you. I started off with the "Posh" building (St. Mary's) with their inside toilets and baths and "glass-smooth" toilet paper. Izal, if I remember correctly, which I enjoyed for about four-and-a-half-years. Then I was finally adopted and moved to a new home with "brand-new" parents and a brother. It was a family-run bakery, Off Licence and corner shop which opened seven days a week from 7a.m. to 10.30p.m. Half day closing was on Wednesday. Our tin bath lived on its 6" nail on the wall in our back yard and was dutifully dragged into the scullery/kitchen on a Friday night; Bath Night! where we bathed in an orderly fashion. Mum first with piping hot clean water at a temperature only woman seem to be able to survive. Dad next, brother, then yours truly. By the time the now almost cold water got to me I think I came out dirtier than when I went in. At least I wasn't put through the mangle afterwards. I think roughly once a month Dad, brother and me settled for complete luxury; the local Public Baths, where we used to soak up to our chins in hot soapy water, seemingly it appeared for ever. We even had big bath towels that were mainly soft to the skin, as opposed to the towels at home which was a bit like being rubbed down with sandpaper. Oh, and I forgot to mention, the outside loo. Halcyon days eh? And whatever happened to the good old Pumice stones, just like a smooth bit of moon rock? Got to go and have a shower now. Amazingly I don't have a bath these days either. Not my choice sadly! Mind you when I stay at a hotel or a "posh" home I take the opportunity to enjoy a bath, even though these days I now struggle to get out. Life isn't fair, is it? I wonder if the EU may tell us we all need baths at home, or not!

KOKO as always,

Terry

Baths and Toilets

Hi Terry,

Interesting to hear both sides of the coin from you and Michael M. when it comes to baths and toilets. At St. Anne's there were no tin tubs; it wasn't until I went to Wales I saw my first one hanging on a rusty nail on the back garden wall. I did wonder at the time what it was used for and then it became so familiar come bath time when it was taken off the wall, and filled with huge black pots of boiling water which were constantly kept on the go on top of the black stove in the kitchen/diner. Did I ever use one? No! My eldest sister Kathleen who married a Canadian soldier during the war, was horrified when he came out of the service and took her to

Sherbrooke, Quebec in Canada to an out of the way farm where the toilet and bath facilities were outside, with a tin tub hanging on a rusty nail. It was a rude awakening to use a tub rather than sit in a bath; worse still to be watched by the other members of the family while she soaked.

Like St. Mary's, the girls of St. Anne's used the baths and once filled with water by a Nun it became thick with dirty sludge so the last girl out not only had to bath in it, she had to clean it too.

Such were the Holy days of youth.

Michael, your memory is good. Ever thought of writing your own memoirs? Group members like Terry, his brother Max, John F. Ron Mulligan and John M. Murray have done so and made a remarkable contribution towards social history. Unless we write these stories, they are lost forever.

Take care. KOKO.

With hugs.

Caroline

BREXIT: Out.

Mmmm John,

Not sure if the EXIT vote meets with your approval. Scotland may have tried to leave at some point any way. Northern Ireland has been under pressure to re-unite with Eire for years. Any excuse will do.

The idea those whom the Gods wish to destroy, they first make mad, may be interpreted by the leavers that to remain WAS mad! Switzerland is reported as saying 'anyone wanting to join Europe MUST be mad' – *Daily Mail*. But, the question is, have we actually left Europe? It seems it is going to take a while before we do. Now 2.6 million have petitioned for another referendum. Perhaps you were one of them. Hee, hee! Will the economy suffer? Perhaps for a while, thus making the UK not so attractive for the hoards waiting to flood over her.

John, is it the Irish who say, 'It's an ill wind that doesn't blow some good.'

Michael M

Think On

Michael,

And another saying, 'He who sups with the devil should use a long spoon!' The Daily Mail panders to prejudice. It is a right wing publication which like the Nazis, historically pressed the "right buttons" to get the masses on side. My advice is find a newspaper (Not the D.M.) that does not agree with your views, then perhaps you will have a more rounded view. Do you think we will have more influence on a future American President or will the "special relationship" lapse and our small island will be viewed from a height in excess over 35000ft, as Air Force One makes a worthwhile trip to visit the EU, the real future power house. Remember the popular T.V. Show "Yes Minister", when the minister questioned his top civil service mandarin – 'If you are so against joining Europe, why did we join?' The answer from Nigel Hawthorne was 'To destroy it from the inside, of course.'

Think on and keep on thinking on.

Delvin John

Connection query

Hi John,

This is a copy of an email I sent to your other address.

I'm a friend of Phil Harris and I found your email address through the internet. He said he was at St. Mary's Orphanage, Gravesend with you, around 1947 to 1950ish. If you get this email please do reply.

Many thanks.

Neil Andrews, on behalf of Phil Harris. We live in New Zealand.

Amazing!

Neil,

I remember Phil Harris very well indeed. Thanks for writing and it would be great to hear from Phil. If I remember correctly he has a birthday in February and is the same age as me, seventy-seven-years.

KOKO.

John

Awesome!

Hi John,

That's what he called you. Awesome!

Great to get a reply back. Yes, you are correct to my knowledge I think it's around the 7th or 8th February mark for his birthday and he did turn seventy-seven this year. I got to know him by walking my dog around the same place over the last ten-to-twelve years and it's quite interesting the stories he has to tell. I'll let him know you've replied later this evening when I see him and take it from there. He did have a computer at home and he struggled with it a bit, so he ended up passing it on to his daughter. Any communication will be through me or her.

Best regards,

Neil

(I too am originally from the UK.)

Freeloaders

Neil,

It is amazing how our erstwhile "brothers" keep surfacing. For almost twenty years many of the lads have participated in our writing group. Sadly not too much is happening now as most of our lot have exhausted their fund of stories but my mate Terry McKenna has collected many of the accounts, including his own of those far off days. Perhaps he being a generous fellow may send stuff to Phil Harris. It would be very interesting to learn what Phil has been up to over the years. My last sight of him was a photograph of him with his feet up taken while he was in the Forces in Aden.

Subsequently about 1962/63/64 he attended a party at Grove Park, London SE 12 and then disappeared from the scene. Phil may remember some of our crowd enjoying tea and cakes at his mother's home in the fifties. He had to remonstrate with her to tone down her hospitality by reminding her we were only "Gravesend" kids or what we call today, "Freeloaders".

It is so kind of you, Neil, to write and a pleasure to receive news of the latest "brother", after all this time.

KOKO.

John

Connection

Hi Neil,

I am Terry (McKenna) who John mentioned in his email and I am also a former "inmate" at St. Mary's, Gravesend in Kent. My time was a lot shorter than most, though plenty long enough for me!

As a form of back-up to John he sends me all the emails relevant to our little group. I am sort of the "baby" of the group at a mere sixty-seven, and adopted at five in 1954 and raised in Maidstone, Kent about ten miles away but have lived in Bristol for forty-nine- years.

As you can see already, John has such a brilliant memory of so many of the fellows and over the years has in different ways helped most of us with information (or where to get it) about ourselves. He formed our little group in about 1988; something we are all so grateful for. We have a few most welcome "honorary" members like Caroline Whitehead, our author par excellent. Caroline came back to the UK on a visit from her home in B.C., Canada in 2013 where I first met her and got to meet John and his wife Josie also for the first time. Last year Caroline very kindly invited me to visit her for six weeks, which although unplanned also coincided with the final proof reading of OUR book, put together so brilliantly by her. The book is called "The Boys of St. Mary's" and is available through Amazon and Kindle. If on Amazon under author Caroline Whitehead, you will see other books she has written about her own astonishing upbringing.

Caroline too was brought up in a Children's Home in Orpington, which was a Catholic Home/Orphanage. I can thoroughly recommend them all, and she is currently writing her biography which I am very much looking forward to reading. She will I hope forgive me telling you she is the oldest of our group, although when we chat I always describe her as the "wisest" of our group. She will tell you age is but a number. I made an attempt at writing after a great deal of encouragement from my brother and with Caroline's wonderful help had it published by her publisher Bruce Batchelor (whom I met during my visit last year). The book has never been for sale so I have sent you a copy on file as an attachment. Much of this is in our book "The Boys of St. Mary's". There are some excellent photos in it which may bring back fond memories for Phil to enjoy and who we all would love to hear from, as John mentioned in his reply.

The diversity of our former "inmates" in their writings is at times astonishing, so clear and fresh; just like to was yesterday. The KOKO we sign off with and has become our group's motto means: Keep On Keeping On.

Thanks for your communication on behalf of one of us.

KOKO from all of us.

Terry McK...

Hi John,

Just had this email back from Neil Andrews.

Hi Terry,

Thanks for all the information and attachments. I'll get them printed off tomorrow and when I see Phil next I'll pass it on. And I have just ordered the St. Mary's book from Amazon. I'll leave it as a surprise for Phil when it arrives.

Best regards,

Neil

Bernie,

Just a thought. He travels fastest who travels alone. I was 6.5 hours shopping today with Josie!

KOKO.

John

Hi John and Josie,

At least you were out shopping together. How are you both? I trust that your move was and is more beneficial to you both and less stressful than previous times. I on the other hand have been having problems with a knee replacement jobby which went wrong and I am now in the process of having it re-done in the very near future (I hope!).

Good luck to you both.

KOKO.

Bernie

Knee Op

Bernie,

Sorry to hear the knee operation was not a success. Terry has also had a struggle after his surgery but I believe for him things are improving gradually.

On another subject, Phil Harris has made contact via a friend inferring he can give him copies of our emails, so let's watch this space. Also Patrick Slevin made contact after a long absence. Patrick has adopted his father's name. You can't blame him for that! It's like saying to Papa 'You say you are not the daddy but I say you are.' I wouldn't change to my Father's name because – one, he didn't recognize me and two, I don't like his name, Neade. Flynn has a nice ring to it. Some folk even think that is my first name but there again Delvin John Flynn also sounds nicely contrived, which it is.

All you heroes out there please look after yourselves. Remember, you are unique.

KOKO.

John

Father's Surname

Hi John,

On the subject of fathers, I don't suppose many of us had our real father's surname. I learned many years later my father's name was Bolton and that I had two step-brothers and four step-sisters. I made contact with a couple of them but they didn't really want to know. I can only assume the loss of knowing me was theirs. I can't imagine you being anyone but a Flynn. Johnny Neade would not have sounded quite like you.

KOKO.

Bernie

Family History

Bernie,

In your case I think as there were six step-children they didn't need any more siblings. I imagine it would have been different if there had only been one sibling who would have enjoyed having an older brother. I take your point about names but if I had learned of my family history earlier I would have quite liked to been called Delvin John Flynn. Delvin in Ireland was the little village where both my parents came from. Another name I used in the past was Deane which was an anagram of Neade. But there you go we are stuck with the name inflicted on us and as you say, Bernie, John Flynn is not a bad sounding name.

KOKO.

Delvin John Flynn

Hi John and Bernie,

Unlike you two guys and no doubt many others, I have always known my father's name. He was one Terry McGrath and my mother is Martha Glancy. Only trouble is that my mother, who is still alive at ninety, sadly is now deep into dementia, to such a point she doesn't recognize who I am any more.

After a sixty-year search I feel God has been very cruel indeed. Before this horrible illness got her we had shared about 6 or 7 years of getting to know each other. The day we re-met was an Almighty shock because I look so like her and I had never seen a blood relative at all! To run this in to me even more we lived in a family-run business, where I was adopted and the amount of times I heard people say of others: 'Doesn't he/she look like their Dad or Mum.' It used to hurt me so much as I was growing up but I never let on. I have always known my Dad's name but the only info I ever got was in the dossier handed to me in 2008 by Cabrini which gave me his age and was pretty much that!

Mother steadfastly refused to give me any more information, try as I have. Now at her age I no longer pursue her for info. At 90, in my eyes, it is not right morally for me to do so. My adoptive family brought me up with good manners. To say please and thank you and not to carry hate in my heart. I am so glad they did and so glad I live by that ethos to this day.

As John, Delvin: Mr. Flynn or Neade said of my knee replacement op; although according to my consultant it went well, it is still giving me a lot of "gyp" when I walk. The real reason of course is I am riddled with osteoarthritis, especially in my spine and it is this which restricts me from exercising as I should. I have found WD40 doesn't seem to work either. Oh, well, I shall have to keep on keeping on then.

John, I will check the Free-view thing if it is still a problem for you. Make a list!

KOKO.

Terry McK…

Hello All,

Here I am making a brief appearance before I use up my 1GB allowance which now seems to include one type! Before it seemed a reasonable allowance, now it seems a very meagre time on the internet to all, hello! KOKO everyone before it disappears for another month.

I thought it was John Delvin Flynn, but didn't you once say you added your Confirmation name too for a while in the R.A.F.?

KOKO, John and Josie and all and all.

Michael M

Michael,

Here is a full explanation about my email address. Joseph was my confirmation name and through ignorance, I informed the Labour Exchange when I first started work in 1954 that it formed part of my birth name. I have just not bothered to disturb this state of affairs: Joseph is now included on all official documents. Delvin is where my mother and father came from and I incorporated Delvin as an email address. It sounds like delving, which is something I did when researching my family, all those years ago.

KOKO

John

John,

Many thanks for keeping me "au courant" re missives. Hope you are both keeping well. Had an email exchange with Terry but it was of little consequence – just a spamming email I'd received from someone purporting to be Terry and wanting me to click on a link. Terry clarified that for me and was equally annoyed. This was not the first time it had happened to his account! Nothing much is going on here. Still enjoying retirement, and the Band keeping me busy.

KOKO to you both.

Glen Cawdeary

Nice to hear from you, Glen

About the band. Remember it's no good having a trumpet if you don't blow or bang the drum!

KOKO.

John

John,

I am trying to trace a Father Shelley, who took me under his wings at St. Magdalen's Catholic Church at St. Leonards, Warrior Square, Hastings, back in 1962. Can anybody help me find him or let me know if he is still with us, please.

My full name if Anthony Philip Standen. If it helps I last heard that he was transferred to Crawley in Sussex in the sixties. He did visit me and my mother in Lindfield, Sussex in 1964 but lost contact ever since.

Anthony Standen

Germany

Anthony,

I'll think about this. You mentioned that your Father Shelley was variously at St. Leonards and Lindfield. If I can find out to what diocese he belonged, I will write to the Bishop asking about this good Priest for you.

John Flynn

Happy Birthday to Tony Sayers.

KOKO.

J

John,

Greetings to Tony on his birthday; hope he enjoys his special day!

KOKO.

Caroline

Hi John,

I am as confused as you are with Anthony's email. I do know he is over here to attend his brother's funeral (he was 88) and is with his son and grandson but that is all I know. I did give him my email – Skype and Landline contacts – if he wished to make contact of any sort. He did send a reply on Facebook but like most of his message they do seem a little confusing. I think he has lived in Germany for so long now he may only talk a sort of pigeon English: and with no disrespect intended, his grammar has been affected.

Regarding Father Shelley I seem to remember he (Anthony) was at St. Mary's about the same time as I was so perhaps he needs to contact Diagrama, though of course to whom he would speak, isn't currently clear, is it? Obviously you have far better contacts on that score than I do. The postal code of RH16 2LE he quoted is Lewes Road, West Sussex, and this particular code is now a Funeral parlour.

Oh well, he has your contact and mine so we must wait and see what he comes back with.

I'll forward any emails I may get.

KOKO.

Terry McK…

Father Shelley

Dear Anthony,

Your email has crossed with a diary note for today to see if I can have success in terms of a Father Shelley. I therefore telephoned and low and behold Father Shelley answered the phone. He had my letter but had been away hence the delay in reply. Father Shelley thinks he remembers you and at the time, if his memory serves him correctly, you were a teenager. I have left it that you will write to him.

He does not appear to have an email address. Plus as he is deaf he would prefer in the first instance a letter. His address: Shelley, Rev Anthony. Retired Priest – Diocese of Arundel and Brighton, 13 Church Road, East Wittering, West Sussex. PO20 8PS. Tel: 01243 670034.

  John M. O'Donnell

Dear John,

Your undated news from Paddy and Mavis in Australia is startling, to say the least. I can only add with a mind he didn't waste time getting to the hospital for treatment after his collapse. I quite agree with Paddy. It's no fun getting old, but we all keep plodding on and grin and bear it. We know of no other way to deal with emergencies of any kind. What I would like to add, is never again do I want to spend two weeks in hospital with daily blood tests done by some technician who think they are dealing with the tough skin of a horse. But in essence, I suppose the bruising they leave behind from all the jabs is small fry compared to those who are seriously ill. COPD, Paddy's condition, is a toughie because of the breathing. There seems no answer other than drugs.

More than anything flying gives one a sense of freedom to travel, so I can well understand Paddy's frustration.

To Paddy and Mavis, my best for your improvement in health. I too use a walker and cane but do not let it bother me as without them, I am likely to fall.

Chin up! KOKO.

Caroline

Hi John and Josie,

Further to my previous health report I wanted to mention that like a number of older people, as ourselves, I am waiting for God-O whenever it may be (Mavis says it will be a long while off!). I'm very sure there is a bloke down below waiting for me. He doesn't have just one shovel, but two! He can wait! I meant to tell you when my time comes I shall leave this Earth without a fanfare or ceremony; the same as when I arrived back in February 1939. I have donated my body to medical science, hoping the boffins are able to learn from my lungs to help others suffering from the same condition.

Also Mavis will not have to waste ten thousand dollars on a funeral. I've told her to throw a BBQ for our close friends and have a drink to the Old Bugger (me). Incidentally, after medical science have picked me to bits for three to six months, they may BBQ my remains and return me to Mavis at no cost to her.

Like yourselves we take every day as it comes.

KOKO.

Love to you both.

Paddy

Mortal Coil

Mavis and Pat,

Your humour is like my own self effacing. You beat your detractors to the punch by attacking yourself first. As we grow older we reflect on our erstwhile beliefs. Are we products of our own rearing? Would we believe what we believe had we grown up in a place where nobody had heard of God? Presumably had we been born in India, we would almost certainly have been a Hindu, or a Muslim had we been born in Pakistan.

We were taught that "faith enables us to believe without doubting what God revealed". Answer one question and it conjures up more. I have offered that my body go to medical science but they have refused it. They're getting fussy. After all the humour I hope Mavis is right and that you have a long wait before you are released from this mortal coil. Remember death is nature's way of telling you to slow down.

KOKO.

Love from Josie and John

Tracey,

I can understand your father being reluctant to talk about his days in the Orphanage. I don't have too much trouble in that respect but recently I have struck on the wheeze of calling the Orphanage my Boarding School, which sounds a bit posh but as someone once said: 'A rose by any name would smell as sweet,' or a concentration camp called a holiday camp would still be a concentration camp.

All the time we were at St. Mary's, Max was known as Philip. I heard the possible reason for this was Max was not a saint's name and so being in a Catholic institution perhaps the name was unacceptable. However, as soon as Max got away he took ownership of his real first name.

Tracey, you say Max was loath to talk about his orphanage days so I have to be careful and not embark on aspects of his life he would not want revealed. A name Max will almost certainly remember is Joe Power and he also has a daughter called Tracey. Tracey asked me to tell her as much as possible about her father and whilst I was willing to oblige I did request she cleared this with her father first but she didn't come back to me. I don't know when Max came to St. Mary's. He did have a loving mother. So kind that Max had to remonstrate with her to lay off the hospitality, by pointing out we were after all only Gravesend kids. Gravesend in Kent, England, where St. Mary's Orphanage was located until its demolition about 1972. The bonds between mother and son may have been weakened by his unnatural stay in an institution without a break for all those years.

In my case my mother parted with me when I was six months old. I was first lodged with a woman who looked after babies, then at the age of two-years I was taken into the care of several orphanages and finally released when I was fifteen-years of age. Unlike a posh Boarding School, we did not return home for the school holidays. I presume Max was reunited with his mother when he was fifteen-years old. When I last saw Max I think he was about twenty-three years of age and he talked about setting up a detective agency. Max had more imagination than the rest of us. I remember Max as standing out from the crowd. Perhaps he was never institutionalized.

The thing is, Tracey, what I can tell you or more to the point, what do you want to know? If you ask a question I will do my best to answer it. I have been writing to a number of boys over many years and copies of some of the emails were included in a book edited by Caroline Whitehead, herself brought up in an orphanage in Kent, and who has written an account of how it was for her. Caroline has spent her life researching her family and has had books published about life in the Orphanage and about the search for her family. In addition to this there is Terry McKenna who has also written about his search for his family and who holds an extensive range of our groups emails relating to times long, long ago, but not forgotten.

Tracy, I hope to hear from you soon.

KOKO.

(Delvin) John Flynn and plenty

Hi Tracey,

I am Terry who (Delvin) John mentioned in his latest response to you, and I was also at St. Mary's in Gravesend, but for a much shorter time than most. All emails that are not personal to the sender are sent to me by John because in effect I am his back-up system for his P.C. Sadly he suffered a break-in at his home and among the many things stolen was his P.C. He thought all his knowledge, gleaned from many many years, had been lost. Some indeed were lost but luckily I had saved a lot of them to help with my own research needs for my then unwritten book. So all was not lost! Ever since I keep all emails sent to me by John on my own files. I never share them with anyone without the permission of John and the owner of the email. Ever!

"The Boys of St. Mary's" was a collection of some of these emails, along with short stories from some of the "boys" and plenty of photos. All with permission to reproduce, brilliantly put together by Caroline Whitehead, herself from The Catholic Children's Rescue Society for Children, and noted author in her own right. Several of her books are available on Amazon and worthy of a look. John has been doing these emails since 1988 to and from former fellow inmates and helped so many of us over the years with personal inquiries about family.

He first struck up a relationship with the formerly-named Catholic Rescue Society; renamed in 2008 as Cabrini and now under the guise of The Diagrama Foundation since 2015. With his amiable laid-back approach to life and wit John has been tremendous and I for one, among so many, are pleased to count him and his wife Josie as my friend. In fact, I will be visiting them at their "New" home next Tuesday; something I always consider is a pleasurable thing to do.

It took about a year to unscramble all these emails and some photos, to enable them to be sent to Caroline's home in B.C., Canada, in readiness for publication through her own publisher. She invited me to her home last year (2015) for six weeks. Though not planned, it worked out I was with her at the time the book came to her for a final edit and proof read, which enabled me to help in a small way. The rest you know.

I have sent you my story called "Welcome to your New Home" and thanks to Caroline she managed to get it in print for me. This has never been for sale so I have sent you a file attachment to allow you to read it. The cover is of the actual home of St. Mary's in Gravesend. I know many of the children found their time there and other likewise places, very difficult to talk about, but there are some of us that do not mind. Not too sure I can add to whatever you may wish to know and what John can supply, but don't be afraid to ask.

Regards to Max (Philip) and yourself and all your family.

KOKO.

Terry McK…

Posh Boarding

Hi John,

Have managed to download your message to Tracey; however this new-fangled computer won't let me read and respond at the same time, so I miss a lot of your questions and can only guess at what you have written. One thing I did love reading was how you now consider St. Mary's a posh Boarding School. Love it! Will have to remember that one. I am so hoping you can encourage Tracey to talk about her father who was I understand at St. Mary's, but reluctant to discuss his childhood with his daughter. It is a toughie but I know you have the knack to put one at ease, to open up.

Hope all is well with you and Josie.

No doubt it is a question of one day at a time.

KOKO and keep well.

With love and hugs to you both.

Caroline

Caroline,

You can check with Terry but I think you should consider copying the email received and then appending your reply, so you can read the one received and reply accordingly.

Terry is due to call in on us on Tuesday to offer his help yet again. This time it is the TV system etc.

Before I overlook it again I offer hearty congratulation for your 91st birthday.

Things are so hectic here at the moment I did remember your birthday each day, for some days before, and then forgot on the actual day. I know you will forgive me.

The reason for calling St. Mary's our boarding school is to avoid engendering sympathy, but should the interest of the listener elicit more questions than I can expand on the subject. Of course, you and I enjoy the humour of it all.

About Max I am sure we will have a good chat via Tracey. Perhaps we can connect via Skype or Facetime but hope we will hear from Tracey soon.

Love.

KOKO.

J & J

John,

Intrigued by the association of St. M's. with a boarding school. I obviously missed a trick with your exchange and would greatly appreciate more info. And congrats on your 91st, Caroline.

KOKO's.

Glen

Hello John,

I have just had an email via Francis Frith from a gentleman called Leslie Fisher, who was at St. Mary's from 1945–1950, before going to the Big house at Blackheath. He was the goalkeeper in the football team. Do you recollect him?

Regards to you both,

KOKO.

John Michael Murray

Hi John,

Interesting message from John M. Murray. The Big house at Blackheath? Is it the Academy?

Hope John M. is continuing with his intent to do a sequel to "Laundry Boy".

Keep well.

With hugs. KOKO.

Caroline

Caroline,

The Big House is what we called the Hostel at Blackheath.

KOKO.

J

A Thought From Pat Heffernan

One day as I sat musing, sad and lonely and without a friend,

a voice came to me from the gloom saying:

'Cheer up, things could be worse.'

so I cheered up and sure enough things did get worse!

KOKO.

Pat

A Hoot!

KOKO.

Glen

John,

Such an expression from Pat is along my line of thinking when things go awry, be it with family or friends or oneself. It seems the way to survive is being positive. The odd prayer or two helps.

Hope all is well with you and Josie and life is settling down for you despite Josie now being in a wheelchair.

With love and hugs.

KOKO.

Caroline

Hi John,

Thanks for the details of The Big House. At one time you did send a little history, which was interesting. Does the Academy still exist?

Keep well.

With hugs.

Caroline

Caroline,

Sadly about St. Joseph's, the building still stands but the status has been degraded. It ceased to be a Grammar School and since then standards have dropped. Of course you will have been reflecting this was the school your brother Rowland attended and it is sad to think how things have turned out.

Terry is staying with us overnight and he has carried out some fine work on the T.V.

I have been up since 3.30a.m. as Josie has taken another fall. The good news is she did not hurt herself but since I can't lift her I had to call the paramedics. This was before Terry arrived, in case you wondered. Sadly Josie is not the sprightly girl you saw on your last visit in 2013 with Terry. She is mostly confined to her wheelchair when we leave home for any purpose.

Terry is really struggling from his injuries, brought about by his knee replacement operation, but he is made of stern stuff and always remains cheerful regardless and just keeps on keeping on. Sometimes we go through periods when it seems like sadness and decay is all I see around.

But KOKO.

Love.

J & J

In Weak Condition

Hi,

Just to let you know Patrick is back in hospital for the third time. He'd only been home about two weeks after the last time and was starting to eat more then he got worse again. He has another viral infection. Each time he has an infection it makes his lung condition even worse. He is on oxygen and strong antibiotics. The lower part of his lungs are so damaged, causing him to be short of breath and make him cough even more, which brings up a lot of mucus. It's only about the last six months Pat's condition has gradually got worse. We just take things one day at a time; it's hard to plan anything.

Love.

Mavis and Pat

Mavis,

Thank you for letting us know how things are. Pat is never too far from our thoughts. It's difficult for you but hopefully we will hear of some improvement in Pat's condition in your next email.

KOKO.

Love.

Josie and John

Caroline,

Have you read the book or seen the film "Philomena"? It is based on a well written book by Martin Sixsmith, a journalist, who knows how to pander to public appeal. The story is about Ireland in the fifties and how they used to deal with mothers and their illegitimate children. The film starred one of our world famous actresses, Dame Judy Dench. I believe you would enjoy it so I don't want to say more at this time, except to say that although I don't have much spare time this is my second reading.

KOKO.

John

Hi John,

Thanks for your response to my email. I wonder if you would send me the list you have of the children who sailed on the "New Australia" in 1953?

I would also be interested in reading the book Caroline Whitehead has compiled.

I will tell about my childhood at a later date.

God bless you.

Michael Gormley,

Australia

Hi Delvin,

I was at St. Mary's in Gravesend. I was shipped out to an Orphanage in Western Australia.

I would love to hear from you.

Michael Gormley

Michael,

Great to hear from you.

On and off over the years lads have resurfaced from different parts of Australia. I can remember so clearly the lottery that resulted in some of our number being sent to Australia and some of us, like me, equally mystified why we were left behind. The lights were dimmed in the hobby room and then we viewed a film, showing the delights of a sunny cruise to the other side of the world. We were then asked who wanted to leave this cloudy weather and live in sunshine. Many hands shot into the air and how they decided who were the winners I never learned. Sadly as we now know, it didn't turn out to be Paradise for all. At first we received letters on behalf of the boys about the fun on board ship, but after a while these ceased.

I managed to obtain a list of the children who sailed on the "New Australia" in 1953, some as young as nine-years of age. These children grew up and were moved to various parts of Australia including Tasmania. Some of our boys later travelled out there under their own steam, where they settled. Perhaps you will find time to write about how things were for you? We have a writing group and Caroline Whitehead has compiled a book telling some of our stories. Also Terry McKenna has kept most of our emails.

Until we hear from you.

KOKO.

John Flynn

Hi Caroline,

Our "Black Friday" this year has been spread over nearly two weeks ending, of course, on Friday night!

I have been checking the daily offers and so far have bought two battery chargers for my new, to me, iPhone5. I simply clip my phone into them because iPhones have a very short battery time. Basically this means if I can take them with me, in theory I should not run out of battery power therefore rending the phone useless. This "short" battery life is mainly due to all the things you can do with it. In effect it is another PC I carry in my hand. It is at least four time more powerful than my desktop computer at home. It does Skype and Facetime and a vast range of radio stations (very handy if on a long trip anywhere). Take cracking photos and as many as I like, on the go. Most importantly it is sim-free and works anywhere in the world. Along with some other things, too many to mention here, I have done well.

Glad you are trying to get a new British Passport, which you shouldn't have to pay for. Doesn't the post office down the road from where you live do passports, to save you and Don going into Victoria? If you hit a problem needing document I can help from this end. After Marion's debacle and her passport I feel I am now an expert in these matters. Ha, Ha! Does that mean you may try the Ireland thing we talked about a while ago or maybe another trip to England? You needn't worry about a "chauffeur" as you know by now.

Better get back to cleaning my flat, then!

KOKO as ever.

Regards to you, Christine and her family and of course Caroline jnr. and Don.

Terry McK…

John,

Do you believe that Jesus died for your sins?

"For God so loved the world he gave his one and only begotten son, that whoever believes in him shall not perish but have eternal life." (John 3:16)

Michael Gormley

Terry,

Can you come to the rescue again and try to satisfy Michael G's inquiries? Perhaps you can notify him of the details of Caroline's book. Sorry about the misspelling of your surname in my last email.

Did you notice that "two planes Tony" has touched down again?

Perhaps M.G. may spark new life into the group.

KOKO.

John

Hello John & Josie,

Thanks for your email.

Pat is getting morose each day. He's been told he has only a few months left. He's been home from hospital for over a week. He is on Oxygen at home and is hardly eating anything. I've taken leave from work to look after him. Also, we will be having nurses coming here twice a week to help out. It's a very depressing time for us. He's on a lot of medication, but it isn't much help.

We would have loved to visit you once more, but that's not possible. Pat can only take a few steps before getting breathless.

We hope you are both well.

Love from Mavis and Pat

THINKING OF YOU BOTH

J & J

Mavis,

We are so sorry things are not getting better for Pat. Things are very difficult for you at this time and our thoughts are with you and the family.

From St. Mary's Boys.

KOKO.

Love Josie and John

Dear John and Josie,

Briefly, all is well… thank you!

You may have only got half an email the other day. It just disappeared off the screen and no means of retrieval.

The foot is slowly mending; five weeks now, only half me luck!

Thinking of you, especially Pat. Our love to everyone for Christmas. Please keep the emails coming. I can see yours but can't get replies out most of the time.

Much love,

Ann

Ann,

Got your message and understand it's not easy for you to reply, but we are so glad you're still reading ours.

KOKO

Love J xx

Email Traffic.

Just a quick thank you for consistently including me in the email traffic re St. Mary's. Although I am not one of the "active/executive" members of the cabal the inclusion is appreciated. Of all the coincidences I'm finding myself spending time in Kent – a county to which I always held an aversion due to the dark memories of St. Mary's. It was thanks to Terry that I acknowledged my short time at the institution – obviously I'm not made of the sterner stuff of others!

Our daughter lives in Royal Tunbridge Wells with her husband and we're doing a brief tour of the county. Staying not far from Dymchurch for a few days, in Camber Sands at the Gallivant – such a contrast with those bleak accommodation units at St. Mary's Bay.

I got the surprise of my life earlier this year when the band in which I was playing had weekend gigs at a hotel in Folkestone. I really loved the town – the hotel was dire (Grand Burstin) never to be repeated!

Today we'll walk on the beach towards Rye – a lot of ghosts and related demons to exorcise. Those damned Nuns Sisters of Charity? Who were they kidding? The expression of "that's how things were done in those days" cuts as much ice with me as did "We were under orders" at the Nuremberg Trials.

Spirit of Woodstock. Great health and peace to you all.

Plus as much KOKO as you can take.

Glen C.

Hi John and Terry,

Irena forwarded a message of where she now works, assisted by a small team. She advised Diagrama has a new address at Airport House, Purley Way, Croydon. CRO OXZ. Contact Manager is Gunter Becht – email: Gunter.becht@ diagrama.org.

Admin. Person: angela.farrelly@diagrama.org.

Where then are our records now kept? As I am unable to trace Irena's email, perhaps you could forward it on?

Many thanks.

Caroline

Hello Caroline and John,

Couldn't let that last email comment go unanswered as I am still here – although here is now the Catholic Children's Society, Westminster. I'm still doing the same work I was doing when at Cabrini but at least I have a small team to help me with it. Just to let you know in case you don't already: Diagrama, who took over Cabrini, recently moved offices. Their new address is now: Diagrama Foundation, Airport House, Purley Way, Croydon. CRO OXZ. The phone number remains the same: 02086682181. The manager of the Adoption and Post Adoption team is Gunter Becht and his email is Gunter.becht@diagrama.org. If that doesn't work then admin person, angela farrelly@digrama.org or Melanie. Adams@diagrama.org.

I always enjoy hearing how things are with you both and with the "old boys". I trust you are keeping keeping well as you can be expected and would like to wish you and your families a very Happy Christmas and all the best for the New Year 2017.

Take care.

Irena

Hi Caroline,

Irena's email is available on the bit of any email where it says from: at the start of any email. Just place your mouse over her name or anybody else for that matter and it will show you the full email address. Her actual email is: irenai@cathchild.uk and her telephone number, I got it wrong first time round, is 02089695305, and of course Irena has updated us with the latest Diagrama Foundation details. One can only assume OUR records are still at Purley, IF they ever moved! As usual, those of us who need to know this sort of information are not privy to their secretive ways. Some things don't change, do they? Of course, I do not include Irena in this last statement.

KOKO.

Terry McK…

Hi Terry,

How true when you say things never change when it comes to this company's ethics. With Diagrama the writing was already on the wall what to expect when they took over. The very least they could do is to advise John or yourself if the records remain at Purley and not Chatham.

So many thanks for details of Irena's email address. You are the height of info. for all.

Woke up 5a.m. this morning to find an inch of snow on my balcony, trees covered, all looking pristine white, grey/pink sky, no stars, but best of all the dreadfully strong winds of yesterday were gone. Everything looked peaceful. Christmassy and calm.

I'll stay home today, with hope of unravelling writer's bloc to work on the bio.

KOKO.

With hugs.

Caroline

Hi Caroline and One and All,

For those interested, these are the details I have for Irena Lcyzkowska. She now works at the Catholic Children's Society, 73 Charles Square, London, W10 6EJ. Tel. 02089695305, which is close to the Kensington National Park.

I did speak to her at the beginning of this year when having a problem regarding a maternity test. As always she was helpful and considerate with her response. She also told me she thoroughly enjoyed OUR book, "The Boys of St. Mary's".

As we thought we have indeed not heard a thing from Diagrama since John and I met them at John's former home in 2014 and I don't think the disappearance of Ian Forbes was a great loss.

To Mavis Heffernan: John has kept us up-to-date regarding the latest news of Pat and you can be assured we are all thinking of him; we hope you are coping too. These are difficult times for you and your family and friends. His St. Mary's "family" wish you both well.

Glen, the attachment is me in Folkestone Harbour, 1966. It is as you say a very nice place to visit and my Dad and I spent many happy hours fishing from the harbour walls. I do remember there was a very good fresh fish market, from all those years ago. Wonder if it still exists? Seems you were unlucky with your choice of hotel but there are some good ones too.

Though I never went on one of the Dymchurch Camps (that I remember) I did spend some lovely holiday times with my "New" Mum in a caravan and clearly remember walking along the sea wall and enjoying many ice creams, though not all at once! I realized much later in life these caravan holidays were organized by the Catholic Church for adopted parents having problems with their child. Me a problem child? Never!

KOKO everyone, as always.

Terry McK…

Hi Terry,

We thank you sincerely for your good wishes and thoughts. You've brought back a few memories, mentioning Dymchurch and other places. We hope you and your family have a happy Christmas and New Year.

Kindest regards,

Mavis and Pat

Hello Irena,

Thank you for the details of Diagrama and their address at Purley. I know John and Terry will keep these on file for future reference, and for ongoing inquiries of family history records. Yes, it is good for everyone to know how things are going for you in Westminster, also that you still take an interest in our group of old boys who remain constant in keeping in touch. But for John none of this could have been made possible and for us to be concerned for one another is indeed genuine. Such a rare commodity these days with the hustle and bustle of life, and with no time to stop and stare at what surrounds us.

With every good wish and health in the New Year.

KOKO.

Caroline

Caroline,

Thank you for your lovely card. We once again are not sending cards but we will be sending a donation to the Salvation Army and Amnesty International.

Of course we will be in touch before Christmas and we hope you have a lovely time.

KOKO.

Love.

Josie and John

Hello John and Josie,

The instinct to send the Christmas card to two special people, who despite the group's intent not to send them, is my way of saying thank you for your friendship over the many years. Your idea to send donations to worthy causes is commendable. Perhaps I should also be on the roll although I do donate to charity in many other ways. Much also of course is given to my family and especially two of them who never have enough food. It is an ongoing worry but we plod on!

Keep well, and have a great family Christmas celebration and a Happy New Year.

With hugs and fondest love.

Caroline

Baby Flynn

Caroline,

Baby Joseph Flynn is coming to see us from Paris on Sunday and bringing his mother and father with him. They are staying until Wednesday. I will let you know how things went when they return.

Happy Christmas.

KOKO.

Love. J & J xx

Mavis and Pat

We hope you will snatch what you can this Christmas.

We will be thinking of you.

Happy Christmas.

Love.

Josie and John

Hello John & Josie,

Thanks for your Christmas wishes.

My son and his family will be coming here on Christmas Day, but otherwise we'll be having a quiet Christmas. Pat is sleeping a lot more now through the day. He also loses his balance easily and has to use a walking frame. The Oxygen helps a bit, but his breathing isn't the best.

His lungs are getting worse every day. He's getting sick of being coped up at home, but he's not well enough to go out very often.

Have a happy Christmas.

Love from Mavis and Pat

Mavis,

It all sounds rather alarming but we have more than an inkling as to what you are going through.

Josie requires a lot more handling since we saw you and her frustrations often erupt in manifested words she hopefully regrets afterwards. In spite of all your difficulties, we wish you both a very happy Christmas.

Love Josie and John.

Anthony,

Great to hear from you and your good wishes are reciprocated. Oh, I don't know if I have misunderstood what you have written about the absence of Sisters at St. Mary's. I left there in 1954 and there was a full complement of Nuns. Talking about lovely Sisters, Josie and I kept in touch with Sister Magdalen right up to her death ten years ago.

The improvements on our living conditions, food, etc, was noticeable in the years after the War. They demolished St. Mary's and replaced the building with individual houses with House Mothers. We all used to wonder what happened to the Sisters who seemed to disappear almost overnight and then we had to get used to their replacements.

Anthony, I had better leave – I hear the bells calling me to heaven or to hell or is it time for Josie's breakfast?

Again, nice to hear from you, and have a great Christmas.

KOKO.

John

Caroline,

Just to let you know whenever I receive emails from members of the group, unless meant for my eyes only, I pass them on as blind copy to the rest of our members. I get interesting emails which I believe go to everyone but the writer may not have an email address. My actions have worked wonderfully in line with this policy of the group right from the early days.

KOKO.

(Delvin) John

Hi John,

Just doing catch-up with messages. Your comments re emails, it is good to know whatever system you choose to respond singularly or to all members, is worthy of note.

For you I am glad it works.

Do take care of your health.

KOKO.

L & H's.

Caroline

New Year 2017 Emails

John,

Here's wishing you All a very happy New Year 2017.

KOKO.

Bernie

Hi Terry,

John's philosophy is sound advice when it comes to passing on messages meant only for him and would be of no interest to others. This way certainly does not cause any backlash which often we experience without fully realizing the consequences. But that's life, we live as we learn from our errors. Good friends as you have in Maidstone are hard to find these days, less fickle, more understanding and always ready to help a friend.

Don't knock the use of a walking stick which I now use on a regular basis. Pride is no longer a thing of beauty when you get to ninety. My main reason today is to wake up, look at the world outside and thank the Good Lord for another day. What a philosophy! I surprise myself with my dialogue of worldly thoughts. Unlike your friends who gallop the trail in Maidstone, I use both cane and walker to get around while reminding myself I am not walking the floors of a seniors home. Your friends must have been pleasantly surprised to meet each other after losing touch and all set-up by you without them knowing. What a way to begin the New Year 2017. Love the story – a happy event.

The photo of your later half-brother, I found of interest.

Sunny weather this week. I will sun bathe on the balcony and listen to the birds.

KOKO. With hugs.

Caroline

Hello Michael (G)

Not too sure if I have replied to your email; in any event I hope you are well and enjoying the New Year.

Reading the details of your early life appear sparse. You were two-and-a-half, the same as me when I was put in St. Anne's where I remained for fourteen-years. Most of the Nuns were sadists. We know without fail the many lies told to us children. When Father Stinson at St. Mary's told you, an eight-year-old boy, if you go to Australia the sun always shines and you could ride ponies, any child would believe it.

As Terry McKenna often tells us: 'when a child was transferred from one establishment to the next, records must be kept.' Therefore, Michael, in my view, your records when you were at St. Mary's should be in the offices of Purley, Surrey. The archives have now been secured by The Diagrama Foundation. I believe I sent you the names of those to be contacted. My thoughts on securing your family history may mean you either trust someone in the UK to act on your behalf or you request in writing the information of what is known of your background.

My philosophy has always been, never give up. The UK Law in 1977 declared all children put in care must be allowed access to their records.

I hope this helps?

KOKO,

Caroline

John,

Little did you know when you started this group how long it would go and how big it would get. I find it amazing all our "Old" friends just keep popping up. Nice to know people are making contact despite the years.

Thanks. Hello Roland.....

Tony Kelly

Hi Caroline and John,

I finally figured out how to download the attachments that are so small from Mavis and reproduce them at, I hope, a readable size for you both.

John, I did ring you as soon as my Sony Tablet, which I left at yours, arrived today. Thanks for sending it to me. It is much appreciated. Must put some elastic to it, just like Mum used to do with my gloves all those years ago so I don't lose it again.

As I told Caroline I have made inroads in the collating of so many emails from the last two years, in readiness for her to cast her beady eye over what she sees.

I replied to Mavis, promising her and Pat his recollections will be in the sequel to "Boys".

Just need yours now, John.

KOKO.

Terry McK.........

Hi Terry,

Thanks for sending the attachments from Mavis, now enlarged, to incorporate in the sequel. If you put the two-year span from John on a disk drive, with the attachments, chronologically, it would be a great help. Once I have the D.D. material in print I can then go ahead with typing it on to my computer.

Photos: I know you have some of John as a young man. I would like these, if he is willing. And from others who want to share theirs in the book. Would appreciate if John can ask our group members for their input to publishing the sequel and if anyone would like to add to "Boys" as some missed the first publication. A title for the new book would be a start.

Haven't heard much from Ron Mulligan or John M. Murray, although I realize time is not something we can always spare for writing. To make the publication worthwhile Terry and John, we need enough material to entice the reader's interest.

KOKO. With hugs.

Caroline

Hello Caroline,

Firstly, a belated Happy New Year.

On a personal level, 2016 was not a good year. I have spent a number of weeks in Florida helping my son to recover from a very serious illness. I spent three weeks bed watching and a further six weeks helping him recover. Back in the U.K. I continue to worry about him. The year began well, with a trip to Australia with my wife to attend our daughter's wedding.

I had great plans to continue my writing but unfortunately had to put it all on hold.

I still read John's missives and am interested that a boy called Michael Gormley has made contact. I contacted him as I knew him at St. Anne's in Brighton. He was shipped to Australia along with Clive Church, who I remember as my best friend back in those dark and distant days.

I am interested that you are compiling a "follow" up to "The Boys". I am back to my writing classes and have attached a piece I wrote for your perusal. It may have to be amended once Terry has done his research.

Best wishes and extremely good health to you.

KOKO.

John Michael Murray

Hello John,

I was delighted to receive your email and happy to hear despite your family concerns, you are still able to keep in touch with John F. and the rest of the group. Taking care of a sick one shows compassion and love from those who give it freely, albeit, heart-breaking at times. We know we need to keep on keeping on. Like many of us, John, you do not give up regardless of the circumstance and it is this alone which keeps us strong. I often pity the weakness of those who have never gone through a childhood comparable to ours, but we continue to move on. I can fully understand how you worry about your son living so far away, which add to these concerns.

Mike Gormley has recently resurfaced due to finding us on the net, also Roland Cichowski who was mentioned on page 45 in "Boys" under the misspelled Tchaikovsky, and who went to Australia on his own terms. It was his daughter researching family history who came upon "The Boys of St. Mary's".

I hoped to go to Gravesend in 2016 to promote the book, which by the way has sold many copies and continues to be of interest, but then I suffered a heart attack in May. However, I soldier on!

I am not sure the direction you wish to go regarding your writing but as you know support will continue in the group, stronger than ever to help others to achieve their goal. The sequel to "Boys" is on the table to go ahead with publication but we lack a title at this time. What has transpired over these last few months is quite remarkable, in bringing old boys out of the woodwork due to the book.

My best to you and your family for the New Year.

Keep well – Age is but a number!

KOKO.

Caroline

Hi Terry/John,

Lovely surprise to hear from John Michael Murray, although sad news of his son.

I am unable to download what he has written, Terry, so I am again asking for your help and what you can do with it and with his approval, of course, so we can use it in the sequel.

John knew Michael Gormley and Clive Church. If the powers that be could guide us to where Clive is living it would give him the opportunity to hear about the "network" of old boys.

KOKO.

Caroline

Hi Caroline,

I was sent to St. Anne's convent at Lansdowne Road, Hove, Brighton in the middle of 1947, but I don't know when I was sent to St. Mary's Care Home run by Catholic Nuns. For over thirty-years a large number of children were cared for by an Order of Catholic Nuns: The Poor Servants of the Mother of God, in a residential home in Hove. The Order had been founded in 1872 by Frances Margaret Taylor (Mother Magdalen Taylor), primarily to do social work with the poor. The Nuns moved to Hove in 1948 after their former premises, also known as St. Anne's Home at 49 Buckingham Place, Brighton, had suffered serious war damage.

God bless you.

Michael Gormley

Hello Michael,

Thanks for giving me ongoing snippets of your movement when you were a child. The details of the former St. Anne's Home, where you were placed in 1947, is also where John Michael Murray stayed.

If you read page 129 of "The Boys of St. Mary's" you will find the photograph you sent with your email is the same one J.M.M. forwarded to me. He also talks about the Poor Servants of the Mother of God. His story named "Laundry Boy" covers the time he was at St. Anne's and when he was transferred to St. Mary's in Gravesend, Kent. Small world, Michael, but there is still a lot of exposure out there waiting to be told.

The sequel to "Boys" is now on the table and we are asking help with a title. John Flynn suggests: "Sunshine and Lies". You gave me the idea of "Sunshine and Ponies". From Terry McKenna: "Sunshine, Oranges and Ponies". All meaningful with plenty of connotations to grasp. Lies told to young St. Mary's boys, boggles the mind.

It is also nice hearing from you. I hope you succeed in finding OUR book via Amazon.

We never give up, Michael.

Keep well.

KOKO.

Caroline

Dear John,

Excuse me for writing to you out of the blue, but I am wondering if you are the John (Delvin) who was at school in Gravesend, Kent. I have your name from a book called "The Boys of St. Mary's". My daughter who is interested in family history came across it in her internet searches and bought it for me. She also found this email address for me. I believe you have contact with many of the other boys. The book brings back memories. I am mentioned on page 45 as Roland Tchaikovsky; a misspelling, something that has dogged me all my life, and it is also a problem if anyone is trying to find me on the internet. The correct spelling is Roland Cichowski.

I would love to share some more memories and especially would like to make contact with Glen Cawdeary who remembered me. I was at school post war 1956–1960. Won't say any more for the moment in case you are the wrong John.

Hope to hear from you.

All the best.

Roland

Roland,

What a pleasant surprise. Over the years ex-St. Mary's boys have surfaced and there has been plenty of emails passed between us. Terry McKenna has collated most of these emails and I know he would send any information you require. We have had our group going for many years and whilst not all of our members write on a regular basis, we do have strong anecdotal reasons to believe the emails are read.

Yes, Roland, I too was resident at St. Mary's from the age of two-years in 1941 until I left to live with a family in Orpington, Kent in 1954. The book to which you refer was written by Caroline Whitehead who herself attended St. Anne's Orphanage in Orpington and is the author of other related books. Several members have written accounts of their childhood experiences. My good friend Terry has written a vivid account of his own childhood and he will gladly send you a copy; in fact, all our contributors will, I believe, offer to help you.

So until I hear from you keep well, and as we say in the group KOKO, which means "Keep On Keeping On.

KOKO.

John

John,

Although I was not in any way connected with St. Mary's, Gravesend, other than when my brother Bill was put in there, you cannot imagine the thrill I get when Old Boys turn up, due to their family members checking the web for family history and up pops the book with memories of old staring one in the face, or somehow through the grapevine, contact is made.

So delighted that Roland Cichowski, who says he is mentioned in "Boys" but the surname was misspelled and has now given us the chance to correct it, has been in touch with Tony Kelly and J. O'Donnell. It is truly a very small world and a blessing the group approved publication of the book, without which there would have been no future contact with old boys. I am amazed as I believe are Tony K., John O'D and Glen Cawdeary. What began as an idea to form a "network" in 1988 has turned out to be an extraordinary piece of social history. I so regret not having the same feedback from the old St. Anne's girls to follow through on the same lines as the boys; an unusual group of writers, unique in themselves, caring and supportive in every way.

Pat Heffernan's memories were overlooked in the first book. Mavis, his wife, would like to see these included if we go ahead with the sequel to "Boys". A suggested title for the sequel, would give it a head start. "It is time for all good men to come to the aid of the party".

What about it?

KOKO.

Caroline

Hi Terry,

I had thought of asking John O'Donnell's opinion if the Catholic Church's theology on child-care has changed dramatically in any way, to give a child memories that do not haunt him for the rest of his life, as being the dogma of the Sisters of Charity and the Sisters of Mercy. I realize slight changes in this direction were made over the years through new UK government laws, but has anything really changed to make the lives of children better for those in care? Orphanages, as we knew them, no longer exist but does this mean all governments still leave the care-givers a free hand to carry on, without overseeing the welfare of a child?

The idea of the question to J. O'D is to ask if any constructive changes were made to the child-care system? If so, it would be good to make reference to these in the sequel to "Boys".

What do you think?

Take care. With hugs

Caroline

Never Say Die.

Before I mention John O'D, I can tell you the Catholic Church has not changed one iota in its outmoded and selfish singularity, with no thought to you and I and they are so far out of touch and date with life. I am surprised they are not still talking in Latin! No one really understands where they are coming from or indeed where they are going, if anywhere. The practice and word of "orphanage" is never used these days. Orphanages as we understood and knew only too well may no longer be in existence, but they are still around under the thinly disguised "Fostering" system run by local councils. You are made to wait I think, until you are at least sixteen, before you can even begin to ask about your early life. You have to apply to your local council and meet with someone who isn't at all qualified in Child Psychiatry or Psychology, which I hasten to add is not their fault. The big difference nowadays is whichever council holds your records (there are always records) and must by law provide you with basic details, but not addresses and names. You have to go through a selected specialist who has authority to contact family. This is something I understand that there is a need for all sort of reasons. Unbelievably, if the parent says "NO" then that's it! No means No in the eyes of the law, so very little has changed in reality, except councils having to supply you with what they have on you under the Freedom of Information law.

In fairness they do this so much better than was done before, even by the more "helpful" organizations.

I personally was so lucky and grateful to get Irene Coppock, allocated to my initial inquiry with The Catholic Children's Rescue Society from about 2007/8. Before then I had spent nearly fifty-years being given the runaround by the Roman Catholic Church. But for those who know me I wasn't ever going to give up. This is my life NOT theirs they were messing with, and at times I had to threaten litigation to get the smallest snippet of information. In those early days it took me over three (yes, three) years just to get my original birth certificate. All I had for tools in those days was a pen and a telephone, along with my "never say die" attitude and a great determination not to be fobbed off by anyone.

Around 2008/9 The Catholic Rescue Society changed their name to Cabrini. Was this the change of the Catholic Dogma from centuries falling in line with modern times and thinking. No, it was because the British and many worldwide countries and their governments, deciding couples of the same sex were to be allowed to adopt children. The Catholic Church wouldn't stand for that and still don't, and changed their name to Cabrini. As mentioned my Social Worker, Irene Coppock, was just brilliant, along with Irena Lyczkowski, Teresa Downey (who John and Josie Flynn, your good self and me met in Orpington in 2013). We thank Mr. Flynn for the wonderful relationship he built up with the two ladies I just mentioned, and who I feel often went beyond their remit and helped us time and again. We all have a lot to thank these ladies for and we do.

The plain truth and reality is that there has never been any movement to instruct the church or any other organization to change a thing. Nor has there ever been a successful prosecution, because the will to do so is simply not there. I think that answers your question Caroline, although I must stress this is only my opinion. John O'Donnell works with children I believe within the Catholic Church and has done so with grace for many years. I feel it would be a little unfair to put him in a situation that might compromise our group and himself. I have no wish to do that!

Well, you did ask.

My fondest regards,

KOKO.

Terry

Roland,

I enjoyed reading your email and it brought back a revival of some of my own memories. Like you about the group, I make a distinction between personal emails and others that pertain to our history at St. Mary's. In the end though it's a matter of judgment, usually by me, how these emails will be dealt with but we have no complaints over the years.

Roland, you did not stay long at St. Mary's, whereas I was in care from the age of six months and at age two-years placed in the care of orphanages until fifteen-years. Like your dear mother I refer to St. Mary's as a boarding school; it saves a lot of long explanations when asked by casual enquirers how it all was. It's not that I disown the word "Orphanage". I will use it on every occasion when writing to the group. I wish it had been what we understand as boarding school but some of our number never went home for holidays or had relatives visit us. Your daughter is obviously a nice person. I was approached by the daughter of one of the St. Mary's boys to answer her many questions which I was willing to do but did say she must obtain permission from her father before we proceed. Her Dad suffers a selective memory and didn't want to discuss those days. We are still friends. Some of our number live in various parts of Australia. Some shipped from St. Mary's in 1952/53 and other dates, and some made their own way. Coincidence perhaps, some of our number were also whacked with cricket stumps. It must have been a sort of sporting gesture. Younger children had older boys in charge of the dormitories and these older boys amused themselves by use of the cricket stumps to dish out extra judicial punishments. It was all out of hearing of the Priest and the Nuns, who presumably were at church in the early hours.

For some reason the older boy(s) considered I was too small for the cricket stump, so I was given the special treatment of the rapid slapping of both ears simultaneously. Luckily I only suffered "temporary" damage, remedied by a syringe in the ear in the course of a medical examination when I was up for my National Service. I always said to avoid boring my readers it may be best if I try to answer questions and points raised. When questions are asked it shows interest by the writer.

Keep well and keep interested and of course… Keep On Keeping On.

KOKO.

John

John,

Many thanks for your message to Roland, who recently surfaced through the help of his daughter.

Happy another has joined this unique group of writers, with stories to tell which will continue to fascinate us.

With Roland having been taken to Australia, are there other "old boys" with whom he keeps in contact and who might like to join KOKO? I hope he enjoys reading "The Boys of St. Mary's" and it brings back childhood memories.

Take care. KOKO.

Love and hugs,

Caroline

John/Terry,

Mind-boggling to say the least, with 568 emails to sift through. Actually, if you portion them into small piles a little at a time, you'll be surprised how quickly the job can be done. Other than this suggestion, you could "import" a young girl to give a helping hand providing she has mastered the English language and the St. Mary's dialogue. All for kicks, of course, knowing the task ahead and to which I may have no fingers left, having to type each email on to my own computer. Then to a flash drive for the publishers. On the other hand you may need to pop over, Terry, to see the work doesn't "fly" to draft and gets lost to eternity.

John's suggested title "Sunshine and Lies" covers a multitude of questions to the lies. "Sunshine and Oranges and Ponies" portray in the mind of a young lad, a glowing picture of fun. If we kick other forthcoming titles around a bit more we may just find the right one for the sequel.

The happy faces sent with your email, Terry, clearly agree with you taking a few months off from "your retirement". Love that thought!

We will KOKO.

Caroline

Sunshine and Lies

Caroline,

You were quick to spot my meaning for the book title about the boys who went to Australia. We boys were gathered together on a cold winter's day and shown a film in glorious colour, of an ocean liner sailing majestically across the blue Mediterranean sea and onwards to the Far East and finally to Freemantle, Western Australia. We were never told the criteria for choosing the "lucky" boys that left the cold grey shores of England. Away from England with its inky skies, to the land of sunshine and oranges. How the rest of us envied the band of lucky winners.

There were no pony rides. No ice cream. No plucking oranges from the trees. Just blistering hot sun and a place in the waddy, so far from civilization. The young children had to work even to build their own church and school, working with lime and cement without what we call today "protective clothing".

Sunshine, yes! Too much sunshine. The rest was lies.

KOKO.

John

John,

It was my memory too! No film or description, just "hands up", who wants to go to Australia. As it was, my mother was paying for us three each week (hence her telling folk we were at boarding school), two of our boys went. Peter Woods and Peter Robinson went to the Methodist Home in Melbourne. Both were "farmed out", both were unhappy. Peter Woods is still unhappy. Peter Robinson, with whom we are in touch, "sucked it up". At least it wasn't Bindoon, but was it better elsewhere?

St. Mary's follow-up title: "Where are they Now".

KOKO.

Ann

Horror of Tardun

Hi Everyone,

I arrived in Freemantle (from St. Mary's), Western Australia on the SS New Australia on 22 February 1953. From Freemantle we were driven on the back of a truck to Clontarf Boys Town. On arrival the boys were split into groups; one went to Bindoon Orphanage and another to Tardun Orphanage. It was terribly sad and lonely experience splitting us all up.

On about the third day at Clontarf Orphanage, a group of us boys decided to flee our surroundings. We were walking along Manning Road, just outside the orphanage, when a truck pulled alongside containing one of the Christian Brothers who remarked: 'Where are you going, boys?' I think we responded, 'Perth, Brother.' He drove us back to the orphanage without reprimand. I know one of the boys was Colin Alexander (St. Mary's) who became a policeman and who later died from a motorcycle accident (he was about 20). Colin had a brother Clifford. Colin Alexander, Gerard Rennison, Ian Fry and Clive Church are some of the boys I remember ex-St. Mary's, who were on the same ship which took us to the Chamber of Horrors: Clontarf Orphanage. I loved some of these boys, but would never see them again.

God bless you all.

Michael Gormley

John/Terry,

Thanks for the communication between yourself and Terry. I think Terry is correct about Lyndon who appeared to surface a while back, with enquiries of St. Mary's. Let's hope we get feedback and reference made to your book Terry, "Welcome to your New Home". We know we are getting "away" from the publication of "Boys" with other thoughts; what we are now looking for is continuity. How the boys fared, be it those who migrated to Australia with the promise of a better life with sunshine, oranges and ponies (this title keeps smacking me in the mouth) or those who left St. Mary's to work on the Bletchingly farm, as did my brother William who had no intention of becoming a farmer. He threw caution to the wind to join the Navy. The only scars he was left with were those suffered through the knife of the Naval Surgeon who removed one of his kidneys.

In comparison to Michael Gormley's and others' experiences of brick-making, another title "Brick by Brick". John, you nudged in this direction, where some of the lads went. Some entered the Armed Forces; others in another direction, to go on and make a life for themselves and their families.

Thank you for your kind comments; most of which belong to Terry, who as you say, is doing a great job. My task begins when he sends it, bit by bit. I hope to take it off his flash drive where I can run it off at our local printers and go from there.

Pat Heffernan's story, we initially missed, should make interesting reading.

KOKO.

With love.

Caroline

Jack's Son

Hi Delvin (John),

How are you?

As you can see I am Jack's son. Mum and Dad are over visiting me in Australia at the moment, and I have read a couple of the emails you have sent Mum. It would be great if you could include me in your mailing list as I am interested in Dad's past. You can imagine it has been difficult for him to talk about it at times. I am very interested in history and read a lot about this period of time.

All the best.

Lyndon

Manifesto

Michael G.

I have a copy of the *SS New Australia*'s manifesto showing all the names of children who sailed with you.

KOKO.

Regards.

(Delvin) John Flynn

Terry,

Lyndon, like just a few others in our group, lives in Australia. I am hoping he will respond to my request to ask questions about how things were in those far off times. Questions represent interest and all questions deserve answers. If people don't ask questions perhaps than means a lack of time; dare I say they already know the answers?

John M. Murray is a chap I would like to meet. I hope this anxiety regarding his son will soon be over and that all will be well with his family.

KOKO.

John

Child Migrant

John,

Michael Gormley is "opening up" with his experience when he left St. Mary's, bound for Australia in 1953. The lads left on the *SS New Australia* on February 22/1953. From arriving at Freemantle they were taken by truck to Clontarf Boys Town and were split into two groups. One group went to Bindoon orphanage, the other to the Tardun orphanage. The horrific tales from both, leave one shivering in absolute terror. The Child Migrant of Australia has covered many of the incidents at these establishments. Will the demons of the past ever go away?

John M. Murray remembers M.G. and Clive Church.

With love.

KOKO.

Caroline.

Hi John,

Sorry that Josie is not too well with her infection. Any update on how she is? We hope she is better.

Cheers.

Ian Finlay

Ian,

About Josie. She is improving. According to the reading on the ops. board, they estimate that she will be sent home next Monday. They put her on oxygen and pumped her with some strong antibiotics intravenously. Her mind was wandering but is now to a large extent back to normal.

Ian, look after yourself.

KOKO.

John

Hello John.

Just a quick email to see how Josie is? I hope she is feeling better and is at home with you.

See, and take care of yourself, and don't overdo it.

I get my blood taken today for tomorrow's second Chemo round.

Cheers.

Ian Finlay

Hi Caroline and John,

I have finally broken the back of the outstanding emails regarding the Boys at the Farm which was too late for the previous publication. I have to agree how comforting they were to those who had left for their National Service around the world and to others still there or working off their own initiative to be received or sent.

The Contact News Letters were very informative and gives a later slant of those from various homes around the country. These have taken quite long to compile but I believe it will be so worth it in the end. So far, there are fifty-four A4 size sheets and lots more to come. This has made me appreciate even more what a tremendous effort, Caroline, you had gone through with "Boys" before I "snuck" in at the end when I visited you in 2015 at your home in Canada. Do you think it will make me write shorter emails in the future?

Anyway, it is now 5p.m. or so in the UK and I have sat here since about 8a.m. this morning, so it is time to finish for today at least, maybe. I know time is of the essence, so may "plough" on again later in the day but if not, a long good day tomorrow. Must see if I can actually get out of my swivel chair and have a big coffee.

John, I hope to hear more good news about Josie soon and I hope you are OK too. We do worry about John, don't we, Caroline? So take care and make time for yourself.

KOKO, as I will later.

Terry McK…

Well done, Terry,

What you do is so helpful to Caroline.

Good news: Josie returned from the hospital today, so will continue to recover at home.

Thanks for your good wishes, as always.

KOKO.

John

Ian,

Josie is home. She is well on the way to a full recovery. They kicked her out of the hospital because they believe she was well enough to come home and to prevent "bed blocking". Her recovery has been impressive due to a massive dose of strong antibiotics pumped intravenously into her body. I need to get her off her bike and onto our tandem so we can work as a team.

I hope the platelets are up to the required standard to enable your medical treatment to proceed. Take good care of yourself and KOKO for the next couple of decades and stop promoting your idea we should leave the gig at seventy.

KOKO.

John

John,

That's great news. Do send my regards to Josie for a good recovery and as I said before don't forget yourself too.

I hope very soon to send you and Caroline the finished and updated emails for you to approve. The humorous reports of the various sporting events are very amusing at times. And I am certain these letters from "Home" must have been so comforting to the boys all round the world who were, in reality, just setting out on life's adventures and making their way. I wonder how many of those mentioned are still around? I sincerely hope someone will contact them when the book arrives in print.

On a more delicate subject we must again think of the cost and try to ensure Caroline doesn't "fork" out her own money (as she did before!), so any thoughts on that would be good. I know you have more pressing things to deal with at this time but thought I would bring it up anyway.

Again, really good news for both you and Josie she is back home where she belongs, with you.

It's back to the editing for me; there is still so much yet to do and digest.

KOKO for now.

Terry McK…

Hello John and Josie,

We're pleased to hear Josie has returned home from the hospital. Pat was given intravenous antibiotics when he first had a chest infection, twice, and he's still on oxygen. He also was kicked out of hospital as they wanted his bed and they said there was nothing more to be done for him. I've been his nurse since he came home, nearly six week ago. He has good days and bad days and we try not to think about the future.

Love from Mavis and Pat,

Australia

Hi John and Josie,

I know I am not directly part of your KOKO circle but in fact I do read every email and find them all very uplifting and although often sad, much good humour comes out of them too. I like to think, John, you have kept going all these years since you were with me at Coopers Lane; in a way I still feel like Mum or Teacher or very good friend or whatever I may mean to you both. I feel we have all had so much to share for so many years. There's a saying I often used with children I taught: "I am part of all I have met". You both fit into that part of my heart. Love you both, so please keep on keeping on.

I am going to look through my photos and will send you some.

Somewhere I should have pictures of a long time ago of boys like George Capon, Nev Poulter and Bannister's wedding, Des Kenny, Putchy (Brian) and Larry Dutton, Jo Gannon, Charlie (?) Blackburn and probably others who were all at Blackheath and used to leave their cases with me at Coopers Lane and come and stay when on leave rather than at the Union Jack Club. I think some of your group may remember this or be interested in it.

Love what you are doing!

KOKO. I congratulate you for all your brotherly love. Not forgetting Caroline, of course, who is just brilliant. I have recommended the book to so many friends here in Eastbourne who have now read it with great interest.

Stay in touch; good luck to you all, and stay cheerful, Josie.

Lots of love to you all.

Pam Spice (Millins)

Hi Caroline and John,

Wanted to let you know I have finally finished compiling, spell-checking and putting into chronological order the emails for 2015. Blimey! It was endless, but it is done. Caroline would you like me to send the sixty-four (yes, sixty-four A4 sheets so far) on individual sheets or I can send them printed on both sides (thirty-two A4 sheets) in the post. I haven't printed anything off yet; I await your instructions about what format suits you best. This way, it gets things finally moving from your end, though I hope Caroline having done it this way a quick scan with your eagle eye is all you have to do, initially.

The year 2016 will be done exactly the same, unless you have another suggestion (please don't say you do). A quick reply from you means I can crack on with 2016. In one of the early emails I noticed you mentioned you would like to know what happened to the boys when they left St. Mary's. I believe what you will read for 2015 goes some way to answering your question.

Am now going to listen to some of my music and watch a bit of TV.

John, I know you are always busy especially as you have Josie back at home with you.

Give me a call when you can.

KOKO.

Terry McK…

Hi Terry,

Firstly to let you know nine more copies of "Boys" were sold in the fourth-quarterly statement ending December 2016. Kindle seems to be going strong in sales. Michael Gormley, Australia, appears to be having difficulty in obtaining a copy so once things are back to normal, health-wise, I will ask Bruce to send him a complimentary.

With the format you are using to formulate the emails back to 2015, it would be a tremendous help if you could mail copies of the paperwork you have compiled, printed on either side, will work for me. I can then type it onto my system to send to Bruce on a flash drive. Bearing in mind, of course, the writing group approve this material being published. Do let me know the cost of the postage. As you know, it is my privilege to meet this expense. I feel it is the least I can do for this supportive and friendly group who but for John's foresight in 1988, it would never have happened.

As mentioned, the manuscript cannot be set unless a title of the sequel is agreed, so everyone out there with a brilliant brain is asked to contribute in order to go ahead. Do hope however, all things being equal, the book will be published no later than September if I am to achieve my goal in having it registered with Access Copyright, Toronto for 2018.

If it is possible to send Pat Heffernan's story, I can begin the process of where it will fit in with the rest of the emails.

John may like to write the Introduction to the manuscript, time-permitting, now Josie is back home. It not only pays tribute to him but to the entire school of the lads of St. Mary's. The book is dedicated to those who left Gravesend, migrating to another world.

Thanks for pointing out there is some history of those lads who left St. Mary's to begin a life of their own, in the 2015 emails.

Take care, Terry. Keep well.

KOKO.

Caroline

Hi John,

This photo of Pat's grandson was taken a few days ago. Arthur is ten and Henry is twelve. Henry is very tall for his age.

Pat has good days and bad days, but most of them are bad lately. We just try to get by each day as it comes.

Love from Mavis and Pat.

Australia

Hi Caroline,

I mentioned in an email to one of you, possibly John, the Migrant Trust in Nottingham, UK do have many names of those who grew up in "Care" in Australia, N.Z. and Canada. In a lengthy document, any migrant child could register their names with Margaret Humphreys at the designated stations; many of whom had no memory of their origins or families. So it may well be that the chap Gormley is registered too.

Ann

Hello Caroline,

Good to see you back on line. I trust you are feeling a little better; in fact, a lot better!

Such very sad news from Mavis to hear about Paddy. I wrote her an email sending all our most sincere condolences and of course sympathy from our group. Just goes to show how fickle our mortality can be.

Good news is I am up to November of 2016 emails, so I can now see daylight at the end of this very long tunnel. The bad news is that it will be something over one-hundred-and-fifty, A4 pages. Because I have done this as a document on my computer I think I may be able to download it to a memory card. If not, or even if I can, I will send you the paper copies; don't worry about the cost. I will also send you Paddy's last communication Mavis sent to me, once I retype them.

Mavis replied to me today, thanking me for my message of sympathy and everyone else. I did promise her I will check with John if he has any more emails regarding herself and Pat. It is the very least we can do to honour "one of us".

Haven't spoken to John this last week or so and as I don't like to pester him, usually leave it to him to call me when he feels the need. Having said that I may well try to call him over the week-end and will ask him about a title for the book and perhaps some photos also, for which I may need to see him, and then print them off myself to send on to you.

I certainly now have an inkling of the hours you must have spent retyping on your "coal driven" PC! what I sent you for "The Boys of St. Mary's", and it is exactly why I have done what I have (almost) to help you. If you can "trust" me, I have poured over the spelling and continuity of the vast number of emails in a chronological order several times. Of course, you could yet prove me wrong!

KOKO Caroline.

Terry McK…

Hello John and Terry,

I am very sad to let you know Pat passed away this morning, Wednesday 25th January. He was admitted into palliative care on Sunday morning last and became worse each day. They gave him more and more morphine and sedatives daily. I stayed overnight in his room two of the three nights. Long before he got worse he said he wanted it all to end. He had no quality of life and the last six months have been very stressful for us. He didn't want to end up in a hospice but in the end we had no choice as I couldn't look after him on my own at home, even with district nurses visiting.

At least he is now at peace.

Love from Mavis

Hi Mavis,

John has passed on your very sad news about Paddy. You can be assured our group of friends will be sad to hear of your news. It is always easy to say: 'well, at least he is now out of pain and you were expecting it to come,' but it doesn't make it any easier to accept and we all know what that is like. Although I never knew him personally, it is obvious he was well liked. I am in the throes of compiling so many many emails for the hopeful follow-up to "The Boys of St. Mary's". Just yesterday I re-read the email from Paddy telling John of his illness and the inevitable result of what was going to happen. What struck me was after all the very honest and detailed description of what he and you were going through, he ended up with this. The only sadness he felt was your son's break-up of his marriage. How unselfish was that and it really struck a chord with me.

Again, you have all our sympathies as well as your family.

Sincerely yours, Mavis.

Terry McK…

Sad Time

Our prayers to Mavis.

One less is a sad day for us all.

KOKO.

Tony Kelly

Canada.

Condolences

Hello Terry,

Thanks for your condolences. Pat fought his illness to the end, but he suffered so much and wanted to end it all in the last few days. I am consoled that he is now at peace, though I miss him terribly.

I hope all the emails I sent you recently about Pat's early life will be added to the sequel so his memory will be kept alive in this way.

He didn't want a lot of people to know about his early life as he seemed ashamed, but it was his mother's fault not his. His two sisters tracked him down several years ago and were overjoyed to meet him but after the mother died they changed their attitude to him. They had told their children of Pat but were ashamed to tell anyone else. They said their mother had a good reputation in the town and they didn't want her name ruined. As far as I am concerned, their mother didn't deserve her good reputation after the way she rejected Pat. She sent him to a Home when he was a baby and refused to acknowledge him when he tracked her down.

I feel very sad about how Pat was treated in his early life, but at least we had a wonderful marriage and memories.

Many thanks again.

Mavis,

Australia

Hi Mavis,

Thank you for your reply email and taking the time out to what must be distressing for you. As your email arrived I am sat at my desktop, still vetting and organizing all the emails I have over the years from John and hopefully to ensure those missed in the first book will make this one.

I can assure you the emails I have of Pat's will be included, as will any others John may hold. This whole task for me is a labour of love, collating and putting it in some sort of order. I am doing this (as I did to a lesser extent with the first book) because I know Caroline has her own health at this time to consider. I have so much to thank her and John for what they have given me (and still are) over the years and in a small way this is my way of saying, 'thank you.' It is also to ensure these stories of the group who Caroline so brilliantly turns them in a book are recorded for good, and seen all around the world.

I have to admit I loved Pat's humorous reference of having a BBQ with all your friends and family and think it is a great idea. I am also impressed with his matter-of-fact directness regarding his illness, and his lack of blaming his situation on anyone or the Navy. It takes a man of really good character and no-mean strength of mind to speak like that. You made a great choice with your man, Pat, as he did with you, Mavis. I was never that lucky with two marriages but they were full of love long before they ended so maybe I didn't do too badly after all. John does struggle at bit at home; not so much with his health but Josie's which must be an enormous strain for him. He seems to handle everything thrown at him with his very charming and engaging manner and which has served not only him well but all of us.

Living in Bristol about 170 miles away from Sidcup, I visit them as often as I can. There is always a warm welcome at Chez Flynn but I have to keep telling John to look after himself because Josie needs him well too.

Enough from me for now as I do tend to go on a bit. Please don't be afraid to email any time if you so wish, and tell us when Pat's service will be held. If you are able to let me know I will make sure everyone else in the group also knows.

Do take care of yourself, Mavis.

KOKO.

Terry McK…

Hi Terry,

Do I detect from your message Pat Heffernan has passed away? I had not long emailed a note to Mavis, hoping they were all right. Very sad to hear of this latest news. Life, as we know, can be so cruel when least expected. Although we realized our friend was a sick man, it is in the finality of losing a loved one which is often difficult to bear.

I am happy Mavis forwarded his memories when she did, and how pleased Pat would have been to read them in the sequel publication. I appreciate you forwarding all our sympathies. Also thanks for checking if there were any further emails between him and the group. No doubt John will advise via the net.

"Boys" was over three-hundred pages and I don't expect the sequel to be any less. Albeit, we are lacking the continuity of stories when the boys left St. Mary's, and of those like Ron Mulligan and John M. Murray who may no longer have anything to contribute. We know only too well how much time and energy goes into writing; however, with "Boys" we succeeded in bringing out of the woodwork many old boys living in other parts of the world and also in getting across to the reader what their stories were all about. I cannot help but feel those lads who were shipped to Australia went blindly to the outback without the slightest knowledge of how it would affect them then, and later in life. It would be good if we could somehow find out the names of the boys who went on the *SS New Australia* in 1953. I have a feeling John may know their names. We need to honour them whether living or now dead.

You are right the tunnel is long, but as you are now working on 2016 shows how much time and energy you have spent in collating the emails but feel you are now at the bottom of it. Either way, printed matter or memory stick, should serve the purpose to your question.

Now you have egged me on I feel I can cope a little at a time, throughout coughing bouts, and see some formation of the manuscript develop once we agree on a title. "Those Who Never Came Back", just flashed across my mind. As we intended John, yourself and I, with the help of the group – Ann (honorary member) who is a great supporter, "The Boys of St. Mary's" and its history has been recorded for all time. If we complete the sequel to this historic era, it is to be hoped it will be in the archives of Canada, England, Australia and New Zealand. At the very least, Terry, it would be good to know where these lads who were shipped to Australia are today, and who we will always remember.

My prayers are with Mavis at this time.

With hugs.

Caroline

Records Request

Hi Caroline,

Well, I can see you have been busy, despite your hacking cough; but why does it not surprise me? I didn't realize you hadn't heard Pat has indeed passed away. Mavis informed John he "left" us on Wednesday, 25th and he emailed me straightaway, as did Mavis, hence my email of condolence back to her. As you know, she has asked if I can be sure Pat's emails to John and the ones she sent just recently, make the book. I did promise her I would talk to you and John to ensure this happened.

I have also read the email exchanges with Michael Gormley and yourself and his attempts to get his records. Apparently, OUR records are now kept in Rochester, even though he still has to communicate by letter to the Purley address. Really wrong and irresponsible of The Diagrama Foundation not to have the courtesy to let us know. They have thus far lived up entirely to my opinion of those I met at John's former home. No thought to those who may need their services now and in the future. Just as it has always been! At least it is good Michael G. is emailing you and opening up a little. If it becomes too much for you at this time then do please ask him to contact me. I won't contact him unless you say it's OK to do so, or he does.

The list of boys John knows who set sail for Australia on the *SS New Australia*, is with me and you should have a copy. If not, let me know and I will send it. Ironically, I could have been on that very sailing if my Adoptive Parents hadn't begun their series of visits and hadn't spotted this adorable four-year old little lad, ME! My birth mother gave her consent for me to be sent to Australia in 1952, even though she initially said she had not until I showed her the evidence which proved she did!

This and so many other snippets of my very early life were given to me in a folder containing things like a medical (including a test for "Bird Flu", would you believe!) and several by now Sepia-faded and former white A4 sized documents. You have seen this folder, including several letters written by my mother to the Parish Priest and the Catholic Children's Rescue Society, as it was known in those days.

My now long deceased half brother was planned to take my place but even he was adopted and sadly died of cancer in his mid-twenties. He was born in 1952, three years after me. When searching for my Birth Mother, Martha Glancy, I was also looking for him and I told my mother this at our first meeting in 2008. I asked her if she wanted to know what happened to him and she readily agreed. Sadly later, I had to tell her he died in the mid-1970s when he was in his mid-twenties. And I have only the other week been given a picture of him with our mother, probably taken in 1953/4, and is the only picture I have of him. I have sent you also a copy.

The remaining daughter of the family my mother left in Scotland with me at four months old in 1949 to work for Genevieve, one of the two old ladies I talk about a lot, gave this to me. When I was young I used to call her mother "Mamma" and Genevieve the surviving daughter, "Jenjen" because I couldn't say Genevieve.

Must say I like your latest suggestion for a title of the new book, "Those Who Never Came Back" and will change my copies to that name for now, at least!

I am sure you will feel a little fitter as soon as you realize your upper limits, and come to accept it.

Blimey, did I just give advice to probably the strongest person I have ever seen or known and who is so much wiser than I? Oh, the cheek of youth lives on then. Ha, ha! It's not 1.30 a.m. and I'm still emailing. Good job I don't have a life to live! Well, it is now time to go so do please say a big hello to all your clan from the "callous youth" in cold Bristol.

Take great care of yourself, as always, Caroline.

KOKO.

Terry McK…

Plain Guts

Hi Terry,

One thing I will reiterate – your messages are never boring; in fact, on the point of paranoia which cause me to split my sides from laughing. Your way of phraseology is something before never experienced by me but more importantly I love the way you describe me as being the strongest person you have ever known. Think it is what you call cussed determination to do things "my way" – a phrase the US President keeps trotting out. Wiser – that's a bit over the top, but in the analysis it is age which determines mind and body, plus the fact orphanage kids do not give up easily and with plain guts get on with what they are trying to achieve. Well, if Hope Springs Eternal, the cheek of youth lives on. So it be!

With the title to the Sequel, I too like the sound of "Those Who Never Came Back". We can, Terry, list the names of those six-to-twelve-year old lads who went to Australia in 1953 to a den of iniquity to never come back but to be swallowed up in the lusty crime of sexual, physical and mental abuse. No words can describe their ordeals and for this reason we should honour their names in the new publication. I am sure both you and John will agree to this suggestion? Do let me know.

You were as you say, very fortunate you did not travel the same journey being the "adorable" little boy you were, and beholden to your adopted parents, although your birth mother agreed you should go to Australia in 1952. I cannot begin to imagine what your life would have been like if this had been allowed to happen. I am still trying to persuade M.G. to allow permission to incorporate some details of his early life and the affect Tardun orphanage had on him but so far, no response. Past torments must be dreadful for him to try and recapture the traumas which went on for years. Another point, Terry, is to get a small photo of each writer and have it posted at the top of the message; this way it gives the reader an image of the writer. Only an idea. It may or may not work as photos old or new seem hard to obtain.

OUR records are now kept at Rochester despite what Ian Forbes said, "They would not be moved from Purley." Such conflicting details keep us guessing! All is quiet since he left Cabrini/Diagrama, perhaps with a view we are a hard bunch with whom to deal. I will ask Michael G. should he need help with his records to get in touch with you. Somehow you seem to have the knack for opening doors otherwise held tightly closed, but the reality is you will not be put off.

Take care. Enjoy the weekend. If you are having a "snifter", have one on me.

Many thanks for your laborious work in collating and compiling the many emails from John. I look forward to whatever you decide to send by mail and hope we can achieve another goal for St. Mary's.

KOKO.

With hugs.

Caroline

Records/Rochester

Hello again Caroline,

I wanted to answer your earlier email because of the enquiry about records. Mike is right about them being in Rochester, which ties in with what Ian Forbes told me. I've just Googled the Old Courthouse and here's the address: 1 The Paddock, Chatham, Kent. ME4 4RE. I understood from Ian Forbes that someone in Parliament said the RECORDS were NOT to leave the country. I also understood the Records were to be stored in a single room which no-one but no-one would have access other than the "appointed one" who at the time was Ian Forbes himself! John may have kept my email from him relating to all this.

I was so sorry to hear Pat has died. I didn't know him or Mavis at all only through shared emails, but just last week Mavis sent a photo of Pat with his two young grandsons. He did look very poorly. When you have to struggle for breath you need, relentlessly, it must have made him want to give up. Bless him!

This morning I was toying around with some possible book titles for the sequel to St. Mary's. I still compare the old film with Spencer Tracy in "The Boys of St. Mary's and later, "The Bells of St. Mary's". Both of them depict an orphanage run by Catholic Priests but they were good films with none of the horrors we now know existed.

Gravesend was always known as a dead town despite its industry and shipping. It was supposedly named because of the plague and whose last victims were buried there. That has since been refuted by historians. So one title was "Gravesend To Nowhere". Tickets please! "All aboard. Tickets, please."

There was only one tree.

"All things Bright and Beautiful NOT", but favourite at the moment is "The Men of St. Mary's".

The one tree refers to the one and only tree in a vast green field in front of the hostel to where my brother and his family were taken when they went as Ten Pound Poms to Melbourne in 1970.

My bed is calling me, Caroline. It's just gone 11 p.m. I'm not the girl I was!

Get well soon,

Much love.

KOKO.

Ann

More Suggestions

Hi Ann,

Many thanks for your wealth of knowledge and suggested title for the sequel to "Boys". Very much appreciate you delving into where the Catholic Children's Records are now kept. It would have given credence to Diagrama had they the courtesy to tell us likewise, just where these records are stored and under whose guardianship for safe-keeping instead of leaving us to keep on guessing. The sham feedback when Cabrini was taken over by them and the total lack of continuity with our group leaves me again wondering how those future researchers will find the support they need to check for family. I believe it was Irena who said the records could not leave the country.

In Michael G's case it appears Angela Farrelly, Admin. Person, is the one with whom he is in contact. At least she has responded to his request which by all accounts will take her some weeks to find his records and then get back to him.

You are right, very sad news of the passing of Pat Heffernan. Yes, I saw the photo of him with his grandsons and confess he did look to be suffering. Mavis has sent Terry his story which was missed first time round when publishing "Boys", but we will gladly publish it in the sequel. Have thought "Those Who Never Came Back" or Terry's suggestion - "The Boys Who Never Came Back". What do you think? All heads and brains make light work. All suggestions or ideas are most helpful in seeing we get off the ground with the manuscript.

Ann, as usual, you are a power of help with the history of Gravesend, a place I have never visited.

Chatham, I remember leaving from there for a ferry trip to France but can't recall to where. The boat ride was choppy. Your idea of a title "Graves End", hit a chord.

The coughing is still with me although each day gets better and I trust in the man above not to give me more prison-looking pallor through lack of fresh air.

Take care. Keep well.

With love and affection.

Caroline

Remembering Pat

My sympathy goes out to Pat's family.

I remember Pat from St. Mary's at Gravesend, even though he was younger than me.

KOKO.

Colin Bedford

Skyped

Hi Caroline,

I spoke to John today when he Skyped me (you must get your grandchildren, Christine for instance, to get you set up for Skype). I mentioned about asking people if they wish to send photos and your idea of perhaps inserting a profile picture against each name/writer, as they do on Facebook and on many other sites on line. I also asked him if he would consider asking people for any contributory stories they would like to add.

He has just sent me an email which I think he will/has sent to others in our group and I did suggest I would be happy to receive them but stressed our group is his baby, so to speak, and that he should deal with them. However, because Josie is his priority of care in the foreseeable future, I would deal with them to ease his burden a little. John doesn't say too much about Josie's actual state of health (why should he 'cos I am not family), but I do worry for his own health. Mind you he currently is far fitter than me and I'm ten-years younger. He knows I am never too far away if he needs help. He only has to ask, and you too, and my remaining old lady Genevieve in Cliftonville. Even my "awkward" sister Louise only needs to pick up the phone if she wants help with our mother, despite her recent behaviour.

We did of course chat about Pat and Mavis and the sadness it brings to us all. As I said in my last email I am near the end of the emails for 2017, so not too far to go. At some stage you will need to give me a cut off date, please.

My fondest regards as always to you and your family.

KOKO

Terry McK…

PS/ The attached photo is the latest on Facebook of Antony Hayman.

I thought you may enjoy.

Brownie Box

Terry,

Caroline is busy beavering away on her second book about St. Mary's and this time would be a great opportunity for us to send any stories and photographs of those days.

Obviously photographs, unlike today, were taken at intervals few and far between but that makes them all the more interesting. I call those "the black and white days", no such thing as colour. Father Healy with his Brownie Box camera, "look at the birdie", was great for taking pictures but we never saw the results of his efforts and again Canon Arbuthnott took lots of pictures and his nephew inherited everything when the Canon died. He ignored my requests for those photographs which surely exist pertaining to St. Mary's. What do you expect? His nephew was a lawyer. I hope we don't have any lawyers in our group (only joking). Some members missed out on telling their stories last time; this is another chance to achieve fame.

Caroline's P.C. is positively smoking and can hardly cope with her fingers flitting over the keys at high speed but she would still welcome some more material.

Hope everyone is well because we must Keep On Keeping On, as we have just lost Pat Heffernan one of our most enthusiastic members.

All the best for 2017.

John

Photos of the Past

John,

Thank you for your email which was most informative, and of much interest about Father Healey and Canon Arbuthnott who took photos of the boys of St. Mary's. It is only today we appreciate the value of those pictures and the importance of holding on to them, to pass down to future generations.

I remember Father Healey when he came to Orpington but he was not as demonstrative in displaying his love for the girls of St. Anne's, who held him in the utmost respect. Canon Crea gave his love freely to one and all. What makes a good book is not only the photographs, but the historical events will never again surface. The world we know, today, has gone totally mad. The upcoming generation of the future will see things in a different light and the truth distorted from real life. May Lyle was a great amateur photographer and today I value those photos she took not only of me, but the rest of the girls. When you think about it her foresight in the importance of taking pictures, showing one growing up, gives us the image of how we looked as children.

Any additional stories the group would like to contribute will make the layout of the book easier, if this was made available soon. One thing I never like doing is putting the cart before the horse, to avoid backtracking errors. Terry has yet to send the material from Mavis re Pat's memories of St. Mary's, to which I look forward. Thursday is when Don (son-in-law) will download the emails dating from 2015 Terry has already sent me. We will go from there.

Take care. Keep well.

Love and hugs to you and Josie.

Caroline

Hi Terry,

Thanks for the latest update with John. The photo of Antony Hayman is exactly what would look good above each member's story or emails. I sent Antony an email today asking how he and Gwen are keeping and look forward to his reply. It's a long time since he was in touch. Perhaps, like John, he is busy caring for his wife Gwen.

Do you know if John has put forward to the group a suggested title for the book? I did email John M. Murray advising what is on the table with another publication so hope apart from yourself, John and I, we will get a little bit more feedback from everyone to support their next book. No doubt, when Mavis is up to it she will let us know if there is anything else she would like to add on behalf of Pat.

KOKO.

With hugs.

Caroline

Family Group

Yes, another sad day for the group to be losing a "family" friend; the like of which we will never again experience but always remember. This closeness of comparative strangers whose only connection to one another is through their stories is not evident in today's society to give freely, without some form of payback. Going back to their early days our writing group have recognized the importance of genuine friendship.

The consensus there is no more pain does not lessen the fact life is fragile and none of us know when it will be snatched away, even during times of illness.

Our deepest sympathies to the Heffernan family. Pat is now at peace. Our prayers for them and friends. Tony, we have a special group of "family", like no other.

KOKO.

Caroline

Apple and Pears

Hi Caroline,

John and Mavis, I want you to see the way I have reproduced the memories from Pat, kindly sent to us by you Mavis, and the promise to have them in the book.

Why I have done this is simply to put them on a system I know works for everyone to read without any problems. Nothing has been changed; they are as written. Frank and to the point!

Pat and yourself showed a great deal of strength of character and honesty not seen too often these days to share them with us all and I know Caroline, John and for sure myself are so grateful.

I never knew Pat loved apples and pears so much.

I spoke to John Michael Murray today on the phone; he too remembers many a trip "over the wall".

He also sends his fondest regards to you Mavis, and I can assure you we will show some of the photos you sent to John in the book. With John M. M.'s story "Skylark", he is going to do a slight update and send it to me, when he has done so in the very near future. If Caroline can use this story in the book he is happy for us to include it.

KOKO.

Terry McK...

Hello Terry,

Thanks for sending Pat's memories of St. Mary's for the next book. I tried to encourage Pat to write more of his memories but he didn't want to. There were a few anecdotes he told me, but wasn't keen to write any more. Towards the last few months of his life he did become very depressed and sad, which is understandable considering the way he was rejected by his mother. It was a big regret he was never able to fill in the gaps in his early childhood.

KOKO.

Mavis

Hi Caroline and John,

These are the emails for 2016 for you to look at, and the retyped memories of Pat Heffernan which Mavis wishes to have included in the book. Any problems when you have hopefully downloaded and opened them, do please give me a call to let me know. All I have left now are those emails for 2017, so far. I will type these up, when a cut-off time has arrived.

John, if you have the list of those boys who sailed to Australia in 1953, I would be grateful for a copy, please.

KOKO.

Terry McK…

Caroline,

"Separation of Brothers" is another possible title. Obviously they were not actually brothers but were a "Band of Brothers", were the nearest to the real thing. I will ask Terry to visit us on a date to be agreed. He is so helpful with our computer problems as I, like you, have questions to pose regarding what he has already sent.

Lovely Pam (formerly Millins) sent some photos which after vetting, I will send you.

KOKO.

John

Never Loved

Hi John,

It just about sums up life for all of us Boys and Girls abandoned by our parents. Abandoned by Society and forgotten; most importantly denied love and nurture by those who were meant to "save us".

My own story of four years was relatively brief compared to the long "incarceration" of so many. I have never forgotten those four-years and how they have affected me and that I too was "abandoned and forgotten", as we all were.

I spent years trying to make people love me because I so wanted to be loved. The truth is I was loved by my adoptive family and friends but didn't recognize the signs. Sometimes I wonder what my parents must have thought they had to do to show their love to me. Love and nurture was the "missing gene" in my life. As the song goes: "Love Was All Around". How as I to know?

KOKO.

Terry McK…

Hi Terry and Ann,

My friend who is a French teacher suggested the title "The Boys of the Past" for the sequel to "Boys". It may be appropriate if we wish to keep the continuity flowing from the first book. I like it.

Another title: "The Courage To Look Back", denotes the agonizing periods many in our writing group experienced when they wanted to write about their childhood memories, with the stigma of orphanage life attached. It took many years of emotional torment for them to open up and finally take courage in both hands, to tell all. Even today, many are reluctant to convey the whole story.

As you know, the less words on the front cover of a book not only catches a reader's eye faster but what it denotes inside. While I appreciate the boys who left for Australia experienced a shocking life of sexual, physical and mental abuse at the hands of the Christian Brothers, we also need to focus in the sequel on the boys of the past who were not subjected to this type of treatment and made a better life for themselves when discharged from St. Mary's.

Your thoughts are appreciated. Which of these two titles do we go for? The ball is in your court.

Keep well and warm.

My most sincere thanks for all the help and support you give me, without which little can be achieved.

With love.

Caroline

Boys, Boats

Hi Caroline,

I think "The Boys of the Past" is OK, but it doesn't suggest Australia at all to me, although I can see the continuity aspect. Maybe: "Boys Of Courage Look Back", just to add to the mix or even "The Boys Where Did They Go", or "Boys, Boats, Promises and Sunshine".

We know of the dreadful events of the boys at Bindoon and Clontarf but we don't have the tales of our members to relate this in the book. Michael Gormley would be an ideal candidate to provide us with the information but I really don't think he will, or in time anyway.

Mavis expressed a wish to help with any future record hunting in Australia once she has come to terms of life without Pat. It could prove to be very handy in the future, Mavis, and thank you for your offer especially at this time for you.

Maybe we could get enough info for book three. Oh, No! Did I just say that! I will plod on tomorrow (Thursday) in an effort to find out where, when and how those twenty-two names on John's list he sent us, ended up. It seems most likely, as we think, they sailed from Southampton in 1953 to arrive in Freemantle or Perth itself. My geographical knowledge of this area of Western Australia is to say the least, limited.

What I have found out about Michael Monaghan and Michael Gormley is under The Catholic Migration Office Scheme in Perth, W.A. This gives me their age (John supplied us with), the date of their departure and where to and other numerical details. Two down; Twenty to go!

KOKO everyone.

Terry McK…

Hi Terry, John and Ann,

Great pictures and delighted to see someone by the name of Tricia Filley forwarded them to Ann. Let's hope when the sequel is published it promotes further interest to readers like Tricia.

The target is September with all attempts to get it in the libraries, including Gravesend, Bromley and the archives in Canada and Australia.

Take care. Keep warm.

Caroline

Immigration Scheme.

Hi John, Caroline, Ann and Mavis,

In case there was any doubt of the numbers being shipped to Australia, I have attached the ship *SS New Australia*'s passenger list for one sailing only. There are over fifty boys and girls on this sailing; the youngest aged six and the eldest aged thirteen. This was done through the Catholic Church Immigration Scheme, to arrive in Freemantle and Perth on 22nd February 1953. All twenty-two names on your list, John, are here plus some thirty more from around Britain including Scotland and Ireland. I think all these names should be listed in the Dedication of our new book, giving us the gravitas to name it: "The Boys and Girls Who Never Came Back".

I looked at records for over seven thousand five hundred (yes, 7500) kids from all organizations of the day and without doubt known to the Governments of the day, over fifty-years, and therefore sanctioned by them all. Would like your thoughts about this startling fact that must be made known.

KOKO.

Terry McK…

Terry,

Thanks for the details of the number of girls and boys who were shipped to Freemantle on the *SS New Australia* on 22nd February 1953 by The Catholic Church Immigration Scheme.

Although I appreciate this was a time of historical happenings, your suggestion to dedicate the names on the book with the title "The Boys and Girls Who Never Came Back", while some of the boys were from St. Mary's and for this reason alone and the fact the sequel to "Boys" relates to them only, I cannot see the purpose to include the girls in "The Courage To Look Back", now suggested for the title.

Primarily, it is the history of St. Mary's residents of the early twenties, thirties, forties and so on, which has been our main interest and to put their memories on record and to remember those who gave their lives during World War Two. With those lads who were shipped to Australia sadly, we have little history to record. The fact there were girls on the ship and also St. Mary's boys, to include the girls in the sequel with little to go on is to take away from the original theme and idea of life in an orphanage and the courage to look back at a childhood of misery, with small mercies.

Take care.

KOKO.

Caroline

John Sullivan

Terry,

I enjoyed reading your email. Must have missed where you mentioned John Sullivan.

The Sullivan who was my friend would have been thirteen-years old. I could not find him on my list, but it seems you have.

KOKO.

John

Courage

Hi to all of you in your determination to KOKO. I think your title "The Courage To Look Back" is just terrific! The title would appeal to me even if I didn't know about you at all. I really do admire all of you for your courage.

As I was growing up I knew so many boys who were at the Hostel in Blackheath and had left there.

Many went on to make good lives for themselves. Sadly, more are now gone from us, but I do know they would have thought their stories you are now telling are well worth sharing with a wider audience.

Best wish to all.

Pam (Spice-Millens)

Terry,

I believe there is an excellent chance this is the John Sullivan I have been searching.

Are you able to find out more?

KOKO.

John

Boys Listed

Michael,

Here is a list of boys who went to Australia on the "*SS New Australia*", February 1953 from Southampton, England to Freemantle under the guise of the Catholic Migration Office in Perth, W.A.

I must add this is not the complete list of boys who left St. Mary's. I know for certain of at least one other lad, John Sullivan, who is not on this list as a passenger, which strongly suggests more than one ship left roughly at the same time, but I was unable to get more information. Terry found John Sullivan did go on the same boat.

May I suggest, Michael, that you contact the Catholic Migration Office in Perth and let us know what, if anything, you may learn.

I. Fry Age 11

J. Garrington Age 12

F. Gilroy Age 7

M. Gormley Age 8

P. Jennings Age 11

J. Farrell Age 7

T. O'Leary Age 11

E. Patterson Age 8

W. Quigly Age 7

M. Rankin Age 8

R. Knott Age 7

J. Lawrence Age 8

M. McGuigan Age 8

J. Murphy Age 12

L. O'Connor Age 12

W. Tyrell Age 13

R. Tyrell Age 10

M. Vaughan Age 12

P. Ward Age 8

M. Monaghan Age 10

P. Thrupp Age 9

E. J. White Age 6

With best wishes.

KOKO.

(Delvin) John Flynn

John,

Caroline has your original names of the twenty-two boys you listed, but wasn't too sure if it was the same one. She does now have it.

I have re-sent the email I think you may have lost regarding John Sullivan and confirmed on another. His birth date was actually in 1941. I am just about to go on line to see if I can find out any more. The trouble, of course, is any of these boys may have been adopted legally and as in England the info isn't readily available for our own records, let alone someone else in another country.

KOKO.

Terry McK...

Hello John, Josie and Caroline,

Thanks for keeping me in touch with the progress of the title of the book. Just one thing: Pat wasn't one of those sent to Australia. He told me he was on the list but his "father" didn't allow him to go. He came to Australia in the late sixties with his first wife.

Love from Mavis

'morning John, Ann and Terry,

With much head-swinging, to put it mildly and from the wisdom of the man above, I would like consensus on a final selection of the title to the sequel "Boys", namely, it be "The Courage To Look Back". Reason: it correlates to the group's first publication and to the saga of the history of St. Mary's, Gravesend. Rather than concentrate fully on the lads who were sent to Australia, whose history with the exception of the late Pat Heffernan we know little of or how they fared in their new lives, interest remains to record the names of those sent to Australia and who could perhaps with a little persuasion tell their own story. I say this with tongue in cheek knowing fully the agonizing pain for some to turn back. For the majority of us who had the guts and courage to look back to our childhood upbringing and write about it, leaves in the mind of the reader a strong conviction of determination to "open up" and no longer be intimidated by action of words. These stories written by those in "Boys" denote how they saw life and the way in which these young unfortunates were treated and who with inner courage, allowed them to be published and be held in archives across the globe. In itself the group has preserved the history of St. Mary's for all time.

If agreed, I can surge ahead.

Hugs to everyone. Keep well and warm.

KOKO.

Caroline

Caroline,

I like the title which looks even better in Capital Letters. I am concerned when you say, 'surge ahead.' Take it easy. We are not as young as we were. You must look after yourself and whilst you want to KOKO make sure you also have a rest.

KOKO.

Love,

John

Hello Mavis and John,

Firstly, thank you for your concern for my health; not good, unless I continue taking a back seat which you and I know is almost impossible for me once I get started on a project and want to see the end result, with a positive mind and energy.

Now Terry has collated and sent me the 2015/2016 emails and with everyone's approval to use the title "The Courage To Look Back" as a sequel to "Boys", it gives me a free hand to go ahead. Target for the publication end of September or with a little bit of Irish luck earlier. I will heed your warning however to take it a little slower to win the race.

Mavis, your news Pat was not included in the young lads to Australia, some in 1953, was of interest. Of the list of twenty-two names I have from Terry via John, one Michael Monaghan was eleven-years old and his photograph is seen in Child Migrant's Issue August 2013 with his wife Edna.

Could this be the same person who visited John and Josie some while back? We have a few details of how the migrant boys went on with life once leaving either the Tardun or Bindoon orphanages. I feel their history would be worth recording in the sequel but reticence to convey all, takes courage to look back, so we may never know.

Hugs and Prayers.

Caroline

Caroline,

Coincidentally, there are two Michael Monaghans and when Michael visited us from Tasmania he joked and said that when asked who wanted to go to Australia the other Michael, who stayed in England, lifted up his arm. You will recall Michael from the "Laundry Boy" story by John Michael Murray.

John

Gravesend Memory

I too was a resident at St. Mary's. I went there from St. Anne's in Brighton when I was about six in 1949 and I left in 1956/7. I was known as Michael Murray. I remember playing in the shed; it was a very cold winter, or going up to the Squares to play. The long Borstal walks with Father Baker. God help you if you lagged behind him, he whacked you with his walking stick. Remember actually having school lessons in St. Mary's before this stopped, and we went to St. John's Junior School and then on to St. John's Secondary Modern at Denton. Two boys there, Patrick Nye and David Stoddard, passed the 11-Plus to go to the Technical School but because I was not Catholic I could not go.

I worked originally for Mrs Grundy, a large woman always in black and who always smelled to high heaven, cleaning the stairs with paraffin and wire wool. I was then promoted to the Laundry, working for Sister Brendan and Miss Blanche.

Can you remember the bed-wetters standing with their wet sheets over their heads while everybody else went to wash and clean their teeth? I had to collect these wet sheets and night shirts and take them to the laundry, wash them and hang them on the drying clothes horses. After school I had to take them to the dormitories.

Names I remember from that time are David Starbrook, Alan and Michael Read, Micky Finn and David O'Leary. I would love to hear from anyone who was there from 1946 to 1957 to swap memories.

KOKO.

John M. Murray

Hi Terry,

A powerhouse of knowledge. It seems your research into the National Archives of Australia and under the guise of The Catholic Immigration System, is revealing more figures of those children sent out than we previously thought. I don't think we will ever know the real number. What does interest me is how many of them came from St. Mary's.

Take care.

KOKO.

Caroline

Hi John M,

Would this attachment be the Clive Church to whom you refer in your story?

This info is from The National Archives of Australia, W.A. Division which takes in the Ports of Freemantle and Perth, PP9/3 series (in this case). All appear to be under the guise of The Catholic Immigration System. There are 1,242 names on this list alone. This particular page reference or citation, as it is called, of 173 names is for the 1952/3 years, although the whole 1,242 covers many many years.

We must also remember there were several other agencies doing exactly the same thing. So who really knows the true figure.

KOKO.

Terry McK…

Double Yolks

The sequel to Malcolm's anecdote was cut short by a computer glitch, and is one of the many stories starring Malcolm and is factual. You couldn't make up stories like this.

Keep up the good work. Caroline, you are an amazing person.

My brother Malcolm, who sadly is no longer with us, was one of life's characters, whose memories are always with us and was very popular with the boys at St. Mary's. After leaving St. Mary's he went to the training farm at Bletchingly, Surrey. The ex-manager told us about one occasion when one of the chickens at the farm wasn't laying any eggs and was losing its feathers, so they called it Gandhi and it was due for the chop! Malcolm came to hear about this and requested to reprieve the chicken from the imminent execution, as it was the chicken's last chance of survival for its life.

Malcolm took Gandhi under his wing (excuse the pun) and within a few weeks of his tender loving care (TLC) the chicken had put on weight, regained all its feathers and was the pride of the run and was the top layer, laying eggs with double yolks.

Regards.

Colin and Eileen Bedford

Eggless Chicken

Dear Colin,

Thank you for your kind comments. As you know, it is such an honour for me as an outsider to do whatever I can for our writing group and whose connection to me is through my brother William (Bill) Marshall who was at St. Mary's from the age of three-years, then went on to the farm at Bletchingly. He hated the farm and couldn't leave quickly enough to put on his Navy Blue Pants (trousers) to join the service. He liked the local policeman who took an avid interest in the boys.

The story of Gandhi, the featherless and eggless chicken who was bound for the chop but saved by Malcolm when given the news, is one for the book. Would you mind if I used it for continuity to add to your email to John's in 2015? I laughed so much as I typed your story about Malcom keeping frogs, lizards, mice and rats in his desk, which chewed through the visor window of his gas mask and was only discovered during an inspection.

Glad I am not the only member who suffers PC. glitches.

Take care. Keep well and warm.

My best to Eileen.

KOKO.

Caroline

Hello John,

Thought I would drop you a line to let you know, due to Terry's time and energy in compiling the emails 2015/16 collected from you, things are going well.

I have less hiccups from the new computer with which I am coming to grips learning what key to press to get it to work. Formatting appears to be the worst, as the slightest touch causes it to go to another programme. But I am learning! During the typing I am enjoying a few good laughs at some of the antics of the stories written, with humour equal to the Old Music Halls of London.

The details alone of the hostel is of great historical value. What you have also written in your letters to Bishops are very much to the point, no haggling, just the plain truth.

I don't think we fully realize how fortunate we are with the enormous amount of time and energy you have given to keep KOKO going. Deep down I know it is much appreciated.

Hugs to you and Josie.

Caroline

Memories

Dear Each of You,

Memories are funny things! The laundry came back the other day and as I was putting it away, I left my clean pyjamas on top of my pillow.

It is a habit I have had for most of my life. Suddenly out of the blue I remembered why. If I had shut my eyes I was back in Standard 3 Dormitory having come back from school and seeing clean clothes laid out on my bed.

I too have been wrestling with my new computer so, Caroline, you are not alone.

John O'D...

Old Habits

Hello John O'D.

Quite a memory you have shared with us. It brings back a picture of clean clothes, perfectly piled, on all pillows in each dormitory at St. Anne's. I have long gathered in other Catholic-run orphanages, the procedure was exactly the same. The strict religious upbringing where you respected the laws and your elders. Today, it amuses me each time I make a bed not to forget to "envelope" the corners of the mattress. Old habits never die!

Hope you are well, John.

Caroline

Extra note from me, (Terry)

I hadn't realized that I too do exactly the same as both you and John with regard to bed-making and as John pointed out, I also put my pyjamas on top of my bed pillow. Never realized this must have been an indelible impression left on my mind. My clothes are always put away in order: vests and T-shirts together. Slightly thicker, warmer garments are kept almost in season form. Socks are kept away from the underwear drawer. Even my jackets, coats and trousers (pants as you say in Canada) are kept in seasonal order left to right. I had never really thought about this ever before. Maybe I suffer from OCD (Obsessive Compulsion Disorder). I do try to keep a "tidy" home and perhaps now I know why...

Terry

View-point

It not only caused me to smile as I read and typed John O'D's and Terry McK's memories of past habits at St. Mary's, but it also brought to mind the double connotation to "old habits". The attire of the Sisters were known as "habits". What they taught young children also became "old habits", to remain with them years later after leaving the sanctuary of St. Mary's.

Caroline

23 February, 2017

Hello John and Josie,

It's our wedding anniversary today. It's even sadder because I found out from our neighbour that Pat had arranged for her about six weeks ago, on the quiet, to buy this card for me as he wasn't able to get to the shops. It was typical of Pat to do this sort of thing, as he enjoyed giving me little surprises and notes.

He was always thinking of me, even when he was very sick. I miss him more each day.

KOKO.

Mavis

Mavis,

I am surprised and delighted to receive your email showing how kind and sensitive Pat was. The reason for my surprise is that we boys had no parental role models to help form relationships with those we love. Even now in my late seventies I look and feel a little envy when I see a mother lovingly smiling and caressing her child. We never had this. Sure we had care but we didn't have anyone who owned us.

Love.

Josie and John

Hi Terry,

I saw this on the BBC News App. and thought you might like to see it.

KOKO.

John M.M

Hi John F. Caroline, Ann and Mavis,

John Michael Murray has just sent this to me on line c/w with attached photo, so I have taken this opportunity to show you all basically what we knew already.

Any thoughts on this do please let me know, so we may include the gist of it in our latest book.

Big thanks to you John M.

Let's see what sort of response I get.

KOKO.

Terry McK…

Hello Everyone,

Picture of Horror! Painful memories of those children sent by Governments primarily to bolster Australia, Canada and Rhodesia's collapsed population at the expense of vulnerable children, many of whom were physically and mentally abused, leaves me sitting with my mouth wide open unable to comprehend appropriate words to describe the awful truth of child abuse. However one tries to remember this era and to fully realize the total destruction of young minds which to this day, cannot be reconciled by whatever compensation is given by the governments of Australia and the UK, as well as those responsible for the welfare of innocent Orphans, cannot and never will be enough.

I can only end with: "In Those We Trust".

KOKO.

Caroline

Hello and Good Morning,

I've spent nearly an hour reading all this… I just hope that this inquiry is fully dealt with to come unto time and we all live long enough to know the outcome. It makes one think of the line in the Bible: "Suffer little children to come unto Me". Surely this is not what God had in mind? We only come this way once and there is no going back to your childhood years. No amount of apologies is going to put it right or wipe the memory slate clean.

Once again, it's a case of the courage to look back.

KOKO.

Ann

Good morning, Terry,

It has hit the fan! It is all over the morning news, at last.

This can only help with the second book.

Keep smiling.

KOKO.

John Michael Murray

To All:

Caroline's latest book about St. Mary's boys goes on at a pace but to add even more interest, will all of you out there submit any photographs which can be included in the book. Naturally, photos unlike these days, were rarely taken, which makes them all the more interesting.

I just love what I call the "Black and White Days", before the advent of colour.

KOKO.

John

Hello Terry,

I have found Clive Church. Thanks for providing me with his address from those you sent me. I have just returned home from a weekend in Devon to be greeted with a very positive letter from him.

I am going to open a line of communication with him and will keep you informed.

KOKO. Many thanks.

John M. Murray

Hi John,

Good timing, as I just walked in a few minutes ago, switched on my PC and up popped yourself. Well, it is amazing news and I'm so glad for you, Clive, and all of us. I took a "punt" on certain searches as you know (and not for the first time I might add) and I am really very happy for you. Mind you it will mean changing "The Skylark On Windmill Hill" yet again. If you could add some of his story for the book and a photo or two, it would be brilliant. I know it may well be jumping the gun a bit at this stage but hey, if you don't ask you don't get. I learned that the hard way a long time ago.

Speak soon; hopefully, and you will note, I have CCD this email to John F. and Caroline.

Caroline is hoping for a cut-off time for material for the book around Easter, so time is of the essence.

I have sent you an attachment which may be of interest to Clive and yourself.

Again, congratulations! I hope you get to meet up after all these years.

KOKO; really does work, doesn't it?

Terry McK…

Hello Terry,

Thanks for the exciting news of Clive Church turning up. I take it this is from J.M.M.? How on earth did you pull off this stunt? Silly question to ask when I know you never give up until you have the answer. Looking forward to how John M. Murray will change his manuscript about his friend. It would be interesting to know how Clive coped with his life after leaving St. Mary's.

I am slow with messages due to having scalded the fingers on my left hand. Will take a page from John F.'s book in future to only fill the kettle half full.

Keep well. With hugs.

Caroline

Hi Caroline,

Great news indeed from J.M.M. I checked out the Clive Church's after a chat with John and found at least five possibilities and actually spoke with two of them on the phone. I then passed the remaining ones to John Michael M. Obviously he must have written to those addresses and has seemingly received a great and enthusiastic response. With a bit of luck we may get another story for the book. Who knows?

Sorry to hear you have scalded your fingers and hope you take precautions to prevent this happening again.

I made a statement on Facebook wishing Dame Vera Lynn a Happy 100th Birthday and Antony Hayman responded. I wished him well and of course Gwen too, just as you would do so. Strange he doesn't seem to write to the group any more and rarely to yourself.

By the end of the month I hope to start sending you the emails from 2017 and some photos as well. We must have a cut-off time if you are going to be able to reach your publication time-frame of September for the book in the hope it goes into Canadian libraries this year.

Do keep yourself safe and well.

KOKO as ever.

Terry McK…

Rob's Memories

Hi Terry,

Me again, Sue. I have been talking to Rob who tells me he doesn't remember a lot about school at St. Mary's. He had a suit in England, but out here he had no shoes. Bill, as we called Rob's brother William, met his wife on the same cruise ship as did Rob and I. He lives in Canberra and we did visit him when we visited my Mum and Dad. I also send him Christmas cards. I don't think Rob likes to keep in touch, though not for the last seventeen-years or so. He has three boys.

I have sent John Flynn a shirt and two photos of our wedding day and one with Rob's cousin and his wife. He lives in Sydney, Australia. We met for the first time last October 2016.

Take care.

Sue

Colin's memory

I knew your husband from old because of the association with my brother, Bernard, at Devon while on vacation. He was very young and as there was no nursery when the school was on evacuation he was passed on to my brother to be looked after, who was working in the Workroom with a Sister Josephine who made all the school clothes.

My brother who passed away recently, would have remembered your Dad very well as his name would come up in conversation quite often. Robin was unique and the only boy under the age of five at the school during wartime evacuation, and hearing of his passing came as quite a shock.

It was nice to hear from you and trust this information will add to his memory.

Regards.

Colin Bedford

Hi Sue,

Thank you for passing on even this little snippet of information about his shoes (or lack of them). It is something none of us who didn't go to Australia would have realized. Of course just that alone, as if sending boys aged six-to-twelve-years on their own to God knows where isn't bad enough, but a suit probably made of wool and in a very hot climate would be about as much use as a "Chocolate Teapot".

I am amazed at the resilience of these boys just to survive, let alone make something of their lives.

It is good news Rob and his brother, Bill, are still going strong, although sad they appear to have lost touch a little. Fancy them both meeting their future wives on the same cruise. There used to be an American TV show called "The Love Boat" some years back. Wonder if it was named after this ship?

Just last Sunday contact was made with another boy who was sent to Australia on the same ship, the *SS New Australia*, Rob and Bill were on. A certain Clive Church, whose address I managed to find and relayed this information to John Michael Murray, who had never forgotten his best friend and written about him in the first book, "The Boys of St. Mary's". Somehow, someone thought Clive had come back to the UK, although when and where and even if this were true, we didn't know. It is hoped that Clive, perhaps via J.M.M., might tell us of his thoughts about Australia. This of course is a hopeful assumption he may like to do so, but we shall see. If nothing else I hope he reads all our stories past and in the future.

Welcome from all of us, Clive.

John, I am sure, will be delighted to receive his parcel from you, Sue, and in particular your wedding photo. We need to ask if you would give us permission to reproduce these in our latest book? It is of course right and proper we do (as John Flynn has always been) not only for legal reasons, but just a common courtesy. Again you will note I sent a copy of this email to John Flynn and our wonderful friend Caroline, both of whom who are delighted to hear from you and of course Rob too, just as I am.

Many thanks for taking the time out of your life to communicate with me and eventually our group; our family of friends. We are all delighted, believe me.

Fondest regards to you and Rob, and also Bill.

KOKO.

Terry McK...

Pensive Mood

Hi Terry, John and Sue,

Great photos, Terry, of John and Josie smiling and the one of you sporting a "peaked" beard and looking rather pensive. I know for a fact you smile, even give a hearty laughter, when the moment fits.

But all in all, along with our friend John whose foresight in establishing our group in 1988, your heart is in the right place; however, we must not also forget John's diligence in keeping all our emails and passing them on to you, for you do exactly the same and enabled you to collate them for "Boys", without which we agree would never have been published.

Much to be thankful for with our large "family", who keep on keeping on.

I think the BBC should take up our cause and give John the credit he so deserves on the Thirtieth Anniversary of the writing group, next July 2018.

(Note from me, Terry): Caroline, I couldn't agree more with your assessment. John should be recognized for his outstanding contribution to all our lives.

(Back to Caroline's email): Your news flowing to each other shows much compassion when looking back to the St. Mary's boys, some as young as six, shipped to Australia. It is a history I find hard to comprehend how the powers that be could take the birthright from a child without emotion or interest, when blatantly endorsing this action. As written in your own story, these children were shipped all over the world, as our various governments abandoned their collective responsibilities to them and their families for ever.

Clive Church's survival is incredible. I know we are all anxious to hear his story, in his own time, and send photographs of himself and his family. Not sure, Terry, if you know of his whereabouts but I know you will keep us informed.

Sincere thanks to Antony Hayman. He surprised me by sending a "Foreword" of Pope Pius XI, also the history of Milton Mount College 1873–1973, which will add further interest to the upcoming publication. The message from the Pope I can barely read, but I am sure it can be deciphered and re-printed.

Take care as always.

KOKO.

Caroline

Hi John M,

Really great news you and Clive are in touch after so many years. I know it will make both John F. and especially Caroline happy. She will love the fact another of our group has resurfaced and is willing perhaps, to share some of what happened to him with the rest of us.

Time is running short before the cut-off date, so if he does write and hopefully can send a photo or two, would you initially ask him to send it to me so I can forward it to Caroline?

I expect "Skylark" might just bring a tear to his eye in one way (a good tear), and remind him of your friendship and how you were "best" mates. You couldn't write anything better than that, could you?

It was my pleasure to be fortunate enough to have found his address, to give to you.

Good start to my day, John. Thanks for the email.

Regards to you and your family, and Clive.

KOKO.

Terry McK…

Hi Terry,

I received an email from a Colin Bedford saying he too went to St. Mary's and he knew Rob from years ago. You all must have such good memories. Yes, of course, you can use the photos.

Rob does not have the time to sit at an iPad because he is an outside man. He tells me he knew a Michael McKenna at school.

Take care.

Sue

Hi Sue,

Colin Bedford is another who has contributed to our group on many occasions and I am so glad he taken time out to email you and Rob.

John Flynn sends our email messages to several of our number, providing it is appropriate to do so. Thanks for allowing us to print whatever you may send, including any photos.

My brother Michael (now known as Max) is a relatively young person (he will be delighted I described him as such). He will be seventy-one in July 2017 but never went to a children's home. It was his Mum and Dad who adopted me in 1954, so becoming my Mum and Dad too.

I am not sure if you have actually read "The Boys of St. Mary's", so ably put together by Caroline. It is available under her name as Caroline Whitehead, author. Although I say it myself it is a very good read. Amazon carry it and so does Kindle.

I took the liberty of sending you my story to perhaps tempt you into getting the book. Caroline has written other books of interest about her own amazing life, searching for her family; again, a great read and at time very surprising.

Thanks for your latest email and I am so glad Rob enjoys his outdoor life; far healthier than sitting in front of a computer I suspect, Sue.

KOKO.

Terry McK…

'morning Terry,

Your message to Sue was most interesting, as always. Many thanks!

As you know, Colin Bedford sent us the drawing when the boys returned to St. Mary's from the evacuated areas during the war. Colin's brother,

Malcolm, was an animal lover and if you recall kept mice and other critters in his school deck. When it came time for an inspection of the gas masks it was found they had chewed their way through the visor, hence punishment followed in due course.

I like his story about the chicken at Bletchingly Farm, ready for the "chop" because it lacked producing eggs. Malcolm save it from its fate, gave it lots of TLC, making it the best layer with double yolks and grew back all its feathers.

Yes, Colin is a great contributor to our group of writers.

Glad your book "Welcome To Your New Home" has reached Sue and I know she will thoroughly enjoy it. When a story is written through the eyes of a child it is not only in innocence, but the fact those memories stored in our brains are told without wrath of judgment, but trying to understand why "it was the way things were done", without giving a child the basic love needed. The lack of love is portrayed in many of the group's emails in "The Boys of St. Mary's". Like a boil it will continue to fester until we finally, "let go".

Hope everyone is keeping well and stays away from dear old London after the awful terrorist attack. It is hard to wonder why the world has gone so wrong.

KOKO.

Caroline

Hi Terry,

I've sent you some photos in the post. Please use your discretion as to which ones you can use then send the original ones back to me.

Regards and KOKO.

John

Will do, John,

KOKO.

Terry McK…

To Colin Bedford.

Sad to advise that John Dunlop has died.

John Power tells us he learned of this news only recently, whereas John died in January.

KOKO.

John

Hi John,

Sad news indeed for another friend of our "family" has passed on.

Do we have details about John Dunlop so we can relate to him in the book?

Good to chat yesterday on Skype and I am glad you have a done a "deal" with BT, when they finally turn up!

Regards as always to you and Josie.

KOKO.

Terry McK..........

To All:

If anyone has any old or new photos they would like included in Caroline's latest book, please send them to:

Terry McKenna, 5 Dakin Close, Knowle, Bristol. BS4 ILW.

United Kingdom. Telephone: 01179535594.

Terry will return your picture after taking copies. Of course you will need to let him know a return address which will not be made public.

Regards to everyone.

KOKO.

(Delvin) John Flynn

Hello John and Josie,

Just read your "test" text to my email address. It came through OK but I was unable to access my emails. Not that it could not be accessed say, on another computer, but I don't have the technical know-how to do so. I am now busy catching up on a mass of emails, deleting spam, semi-spam and keeping and reading the St. Mary's blogs. It's a fairly big task as I think there were around 500 in the "Inbox".

System is fine now, thank goodness.

Great to hear Caroline is undertaking a new book with, we hope, plenty of photos. It is something to which we look forward.

I just read that Josie had been in hospital and was discharged and is now back at home; but it is about as far as I have gone. Hope all is well with you, and family who live near your old address and, of course, in your new home.

Have a happy day John and Josie.

KOKO.

Michael M

Nice to hear from you, Michael,

Things have been a bit hectic since we moved to Sidcup and we now reside with likewise, old people.

France for the Continent: Sidcup for the incontinent!

Like us you appear to be busy but I note you are still receiving emails from us. When we first moved here a year ago we didn't have Internet so I had to use the Library. It's hard to believe we have been here a year now. Terry McKenna comes to see us occasionally and I will copy this to him so that he knows you are well.

Caroline's latest book is at an advanced stage, so if you have any photos they can be used in the book.

KOKO.

Josie and John

Hi Bernie Francis,

I think Ferback is the nearest pronunciation but Michael Murray can say it even if he can't spell it.

Michael M. was a loyal friend to Freddy and kept visiting right to the end of Freddy's illness. Without keeping in touch with some of our "brothers" they can fade from our memory. In this respect I had an enjoyable chat with Tony Sayers yesterday, when he trotted out a number of names, shown below:

Michael Scalon, Jack Norman (Port Said), McGuiness, Heffernan (HMS Bulwark), Joe Power and John Dunlop. Jackie Howard: and there were many others.

Tony Sayers is really a great guy. His hobby is restoring old Triumph motor cycles, particularly those dating back to the fifties. He loves his cruise, including the ambience of the dress code. He says that after every day wearing durable working clothes it is a delight to dress up for the "special" occasions.

Mavis kindly sent the "Order of Service" held for Pat Heffernan to mark his lifetime membership of the Submariners Association. Pat was rightly proud of his service in the submarine part of the Royal Navy and regale us with his stories.

Pat Heffernan, like Tony Sayers, also knew how to present himself for the special occasion, particularly with regard to his Naval Reunions.

I sent Terry McKenna some news round robins from the fifties and it was interesting to see some of the names from 1955.

Pat Heffernan now in the Navy at his base HMS Ocean.

Jimmy Florio.

Jack Norman – Parachute Regiment.

Tom Sayers – from his base at Saighton Camp, Cheshire, and talk about him joining the Military Police and how he's already reached the dizzy height of 6 foot two inches.

Sig. Sheridan talks about the prospects of becoming a full Corporal.

A letter from Father Arbuthnott mentioning the sadness suffered re the death by drowning of Alan Burgess.

Gnr. Burns writing from the Officers Mess in BOAR15.

Other names mentioned:

Derek Aylett, Mike Sheridan, John Howard, Frank Dennis, Brian Johnson (cricket commentator) Joe Power, Mr. Dill, Mr. Loveman, Mr. Lawrence, Dennis Conway, John Kelly, Sig. Lynch, Vincent McCarthy, Derek Harwood, Terry Graham, Terry Hughes, Teddy McDermott.

Those were the days, my friends, we thought they would never end but I include in this missive some of the names of our "brothers" from times gone by.

I must go as I have lots of duties still to perform today.

KOKO.

(Delvin) John Flynn.

Note:

These emails from the "network" of the old boys of St. Mary's are indicative to the era of the nineteen twenties on… The group of writers who over the years lived in England, Canada, Australia, Germany and other parts of the world have contributed greatly to the "network" and related their stories with honesty, sincerity and a frankness to tell "the way things were done in those days". This tight-knit camaraderie of friendship, is second to none.

As the famous Ernest Hemingway once quoted: "Go for the jugular. If something scary comes up, go for it. That's where the energy is. Otherwise, you'll spend all your time writing around whatever makes you nervous. It will probably be abstract, bland writing because you're avoiding the truth".

Hemingway said, 'Write hard and clear about what hurts. Don't avoid it. It has all the energy. Don't worry, no one ever died of it. You might cry or laugh, but not die.'

Since Terry McKenna had forwarded the emails from 2016 to the early part of 2017, many of those in our writing group continue to message me on a regular basis. Apart from meeting Terry in 2015 and (Delvin) John Flynn once again, at the Orpington Reunion in 2015, these emails did not go through the normal channel of communication yet I am convinced at some point they reached the "network".

Steam Trains

By Michael M. A prolific writer and with much humour sent the following:

Memory of song sung in the Infants Class and taught by a formidable woman named Babs or Barbara.

"Let's all go a-riding in a railway train

Puffing into tunnels

Puffing out again.

I'm the engine driver

You see my face is black

You need not be the least afraid

I'll bring you safely back.

So..........................

Let's all go a-riding in a railway train

Puffing into tunnels

Puffing out again".

Memory of the Woods

One day as he walked through the woods when he returned from a shop, Michael remembered singing this delightful song during a singing lesson at St. Mary's.

The wood, the woods so fresh and green

and bluebells are blooming in glorious sheen

The treetops laugh, and my heart laughs too.

Joy and delight, thrill me through and thro'

In the woods, so cool and fragrant

Now sings thro' the darkness of the evening psalm.

The voice of night whispers "day is done"
Homeward we go, yet even still
Joy and delightful fill my memory through
Of the woods, so cool and fragrant.

~ Author unknown

Apples, Apples

One naughty night a few of us boys slipped out of the dormitory in the quiet of night in our pyjamas. We headed for the garden where Mr. Bus grew vegetables, flowers and apples for the Home. Our target was the apples. Beautiful tasting apples on well-tended trees.

It was not something we did regularly, but an isolated occasion; a spur of the moment decision, an exciting adventure. Unfortunately, I don't remember the outcome, but I think there was an assembly next day and an inquisition to find the culprits.

Michael M

Jam Licking

As I was consuming my morning porridge (Dennis the cockatiel has a small portion too), it came to my mind of breakfast at St. Mary's. The infants had small tables with four sitting along it. One boy was given responsibility to serve the three others with what was on the table.

Breakfast sometime consisted of bread and jam on toast. I remember one boy who used to spread the marg on toast, then the jam, and lick it before passing it on to us other three (it still tasted nice and sweet), and if we thought it was odd, we weren't going to do without our breakfast.

No wonder St. Mary's boys smile a lot. (Don't choke on your toast if you are reading this at breakfast).

Michael M

May 17/2017

Reply

Best laugh of the day reading your memory of breakfast at St. Mary's of bread and jam on toast.

Imagination runs riot, going back to the days of St. Anne's refectory when mine was bread and marg. Jam! I never heard of it, and for that matter cheese and bananas did not touch my taste buds until I reached the glorious age of sixteen. Even then with war rations, what else did we eat after standing in a lineup to be fortunate to buy an orange (perhaps older than the one left in our Christmas stocking at the end of the bed) and only to find the supply had run out until goodness knows when new stock would arrive.

Caroline

Postscript from Michael

The jam was thickly spread on the toast so the slightly older boy in charge of serving out the food, used his tongue to reduce the amount of jam and at the same time, enjoy the perks of the job.

Memory of Gravesend

Founded in 1872 by Frances Margaret Taylor (later Mother Magdalen Taylor), Social Worker for the Poor, the Catholic Order – The Poor Servants of the Mother of God – their residential home in Landsdowne Road, Hove, the Nuns moved to Hove, Sussex after their former premises known as St. Anne's Home at 49 Buckingham Place, suffered serious war damage.

At the age of two, my mother left me at St. Anne's in Brighton, Sussex. I stayed there until I reached the age of five or six in 1949. I left in 1956/57. At that time I was known as Michael Murray. I remember playing in the shed. It was very cold in winter, or going up to the Squares to play. The long Borstal walks with Father Baker; God help you if you got behind him, he whacked you with his walking stick.

Remember only having school lessons in St. Mary's. Apparently this stopped and the boys went to St. John's Junior School and then on to St. John's Secondary Modern at Denton.

I had reached the age of 8 years and remember Father Stinson at St. Mary's, who asked if we would like to go to Australia where there is plenty of sunshine and we could ride ponies.

John M.M.

Bindoon/Tardun

I arrived in Freemantle from St. Mary's to Western Australia on the *SS New Australia* on February 22/1953. From Freemantle we were taken on the back of a truck to Clontarf Boys Town. On arrival the boys were split up into groups. One group went to Bindoon Orphanage and another group went to Tardun. It was a terribly sad and lonely experience, splitting us up. I loved some of those boys and I would never see them again.

"Chamber of Horror", a suggested title for the sequel to "The Boys of St. Mary's".

HISTORY OF CLONTARF

Clontarf was established by the Christian Brothers from 1901 and known as Subiaco Boys Orphanage. Its first residents Clontartf took in, were boys between the age of twelve-to-sixteen who came from various backgrounds including Australian-born and Wards of the State.

From 1947 to 1966 Child Migrants from the United Kingdom and Malta were admitted.

Clontarf closed in 1983 and later became Clontarf Aboriginal College.

Bible Verses about Perseverance

"Perseverance is vital to growing in your faith, and God wants his people to persevere no matter what happens, so we have to come to learn how to overcome obstacles, trials and tribulations to experience victory in Christ".

Powerless Little Boy

Yes, I agree with you, Diagrama has considered me like a powerless little boy, who would be overwhelmed if they saw his childhood history.

I had no problem getting my history (St. Anne's Convent) from England a few years ago.

They (Christian Brothers) did not like the children, probably because we were English/Irish. Also they felt we had been corrupted sexually because we had been in orphanages in England. I imagine about half the Brother were paedophiles.

Michael Gormley

Malcolm's Ossie

Among the many pets in Malcolm's menagerie he kept a pigeon he called Ossie, who would fly through the classroom window during school lessons and perch on the black board. Poor Ossie came to an unfortunate end when a boy accidentally dropped a desk top on Ossie's head and he immediately died.

This was a sad end to a pet who was a friend to many of the boys. I think if you could compare this story with the Birdman of Alcatraze, you could say Malcolm was the Birdman of St. Mary's.

Colin Bedford

EPILOGUE

BY CAROLINE WHITEHEAD

The stories by the writing group of the old boys of St. Mary's "network" recapture a time when a decision was made through the Catholic System and the British Government of the day in 1952/53 to migrate young children from Orphanages and Homes; its sole purpose to increase the population of Commonwealth countries.

In so doing the boys from St. Mary's, one only five-years-old, were encouraged by Catholic Priests and Nuns to go to Australia, Canada and other parts of the Commonwealth, with promises of sunshine, oranges and ponies. Little did these young boys realize what lay ahead of them when sailing on the *SS New Australia* in the mid-fifties, to a country worlds apart from their place of birth, and who were never to come back.

Of those St. Mary's boys shipped as child migrants to Western Australia, two have surfaced out of the twenty-two names recorded when hearing *The Boys of St. Mary's* book was published in 2015 by Agio Publishing House in Victoria, B.C. Canada. One of whom is Michael Gormley, who regularly messages through the "network" and has graciously allowed his experience of life in an Australian orphanage to be reproduced under the title "Child Migrant", and other emails.

It is with a sadness, bearing in mind what this group member experienced when he was just a young boy and shipped to Tardun Orphanage at Freemantle, Western Australia without care or thought of his well-being, and his frustration over many months in trying to obtain his family records from the archives of The Diagrama Foundation.

Prior to being put in St. Mary's in Gravesend, Michael was sent to St. Anne's Home in Brighton, Sussex. Throughout the years when he applied to England for his childhood records, little time was wasted in giving him the information he requested. Since December 2016, he has approached The Diagrama Foundation, now the holders of OUR records, for his personal file. Up to June 1/2017, and much correspondence going back and forth, Diagrama have unfairly been too long in coming to closure with his request despite The British Parliament Act in 1974 stating all children put in care have the right to The Freedom of Information.

Michael has conveyed how his request is being handled by Diagrama, who firstly acknowledged his file had been found, then required of him to find an Adoption Agency in Western Australia to confirm he was bona fide as the person wanting this information. This in itself is understandable, bearing in mind Diagrama are the safe-keepers of OUR Records and need to protect not only themselves from prosecution but also the records of those children put in orphanages who were under the care of the Catholic Children's Society.

It was made abundantly clear to the KOKO group from the beginning when Diagrama took over OUR records from Cabrini, the kind of uncaring and lack of understanding of children put in care when this transaction between these two parties was finalized in 2015. The foreseeable outcome was all too evident, despite assurances there would be transparency, openness and accessibility to OUR files.

The inconsequential question why these files were not handed over to each individual concerned before the takeover from one establishment to another, as did many others Homes who held the records of children in care, will continue to puzzle the KOKO group. According to one of our honorary members, this was the way it was done when these Homes ceased to exist. It is a far cry from the days of Joe Lyons, Archivist of the records of the Catholic Children's Society, who bent over backwards to give his full support and time to anyone looking for his/her personal records, then held at Purley, Surrey.

This lack of communication with Diagrama to finalize Michael Gormley's request for information of his personal file, is indicative to which part of their mandate is of more importance to them.

On behalf of (Delvin) John Flynn, Terry McKenna has generously given his energy and time to assist this group member in obtaining his family history through contact with Angela Farrelly, Admin Person at Diagrama, also Melanie Adams of Adoption Team, with little result so far in producing this file. An email to the manager, Gunter Becht of Adoption and Post Adoption, fell on deaf ears or, to give the benefit of doubt, passed this concern or lack of communication, over to staff who while corresponding with the inquirer now appear to address him more friendly than before, perhaps due to receiving a copy of the email sent to Mr. Becht. It is to be hoped during this intervening time, not only to obtain satisfaction from Diagrama, but for them to understand the importance of any one of our group members of the "network" who wish to know the history of his family background and should be given the courtesy of transparency, openness and accessibility as assured by those when the transfer of Orphanage records were passed from one establishment to the other, without going through the hassle Michael G. has endured these past months and to realize the need to know their background, to which they are entitled. In hindsight, to allow them to understand themselves.

No man should ever be made to feel "a powerless little boy".

The emails dating back to 2015 to early 2017 from the KOKO writing group old boys "network", written from childhood memories, some of which were merited good, others where the lack of love and care were to remain with many of them for years, are now able to put the stigma of a childhood upbringing behind them. In so doing, by publishing earlier emails in "The Boys of St. Mary's" written with truth, pathos and humour it has resulted in many of the old boys living in different parts of the world to come forward, when hearing about the book.

Not only has the "network" preserved the history of St. Mary's and its beginnings, but also it has provided an outlet to those young shoulders on which for many years held the demons of the past. No longer hidden from the public eye but by telling their stories and having them published, the old boys of St. Mary's have "opened" up to the world with the courage to look back and speak of their childhood upbringing in the twentieth century where there was no love or care, to write about them and finally to find peace.

Today, the "network" of St. Mary's is strong as ever since (Delvin) John Flynn put together an idea nearly thirty years ago to bring back the old boys worldwide, and to develop a "family" relationship to which every group member supports, loves and shares without reservation, to keep alive their motto

KOKO, keep on keeping on.

To (Delvin) John Flynn – we owe so much!

Without courage there cannot be truth,
and without truth there can be no other virtue.

~ Scott

ABOUT THE EDITOR

CAROLINE WHITEHEAD was born in London, England, and raised in an orphanage in Kent. Knowing the importance of family relationships, she pushed forward for forty years to discover her brothers' and sisters' identities, overcoming many obstacles so the siblings could experience those ties – and their stories could finally be told in a sequence of three books.

Married in 1944, she emigrated to Canada in 1967 and lived in Ontario before moving to British Columbia in 1987. Her husband died in 1999. She has one daughter, three grandchildren, two great-grandchildren, and a wealth of proud memories.

Milton Keynes UK
Ingram Content Group UK Ltd.
UKHW022338030324
438776UK00013B/1997